CONTENTS

HOMESCHOOLING FAQs ☆ ☆ ☆

101 QUESTIONS EVERY HOMESCHOOLING PARENT SHOULD ASK

Tamra Orr

LEARNINGEXPRESS®

NEW YORK

Library of Congress Cataloging-in-Publication Data
Homeschooling FAQS : 101 questions every homeschooling parent should ask.
    p.   cm.
    ISBN-13: 978-1-57685-760-1 (pbk. : alk. paper)
    ISBN-10: 1-57685-760-3 (pbk. : alk. paper)   1. Home schooling—United
States—Miscellanea.   I. LearningExpress (Organization)
    LC40.H6414 2010
    371.04'2—dc22

                                                                2009051205

Printed in the United States of America

9 8 7 6 5 4 3 2 1

First Edition

ISBN 978-1-57685-760-1

For more information or to place an order, contact LearningExpress at:
    2 Rector Street
    26th Floor
    New York, NY 10006

Or visit us at:
    www.learnatest.com

ABOUT THE AUTHOR

TAMRA ORR HAS been homeschooling for over 25 years. Her four children have all been homeschooled since birth. She is the author of *A Parent's Guide to Homeschooling*; *After Homeschool: 15 Home-schoolers Out in the Real World*; *Asking Questions, Finding Answers: A Parent's Journey through Homeschooling*; and *Homeschoolers on the Internet*. Orr has taught multiple classes at homeschooling conferences and has gone on television and radio to do presentations about home education. She lives in the Pacific Northwest and is counting the days until she gets to help homeschool her grandchildren.

INTRODUCTION

A child does not have to be motivated to learn; in fact, learning cannot be stopped. A child will focus on the world around him and long to understand it. He will want to know why things are the way that they are. He won't have to be told to be curious; he will just be curious. He has no desire to be ignorant; rather he wants to know everything. But he wants to discover his interests on his own. He doesn't want to be pushed into learning what others think he should know. He wants to sample all that is in front of him and find his own destiny. Without interference he will do just that.

—Valerie Fitzenreiter, *The Unprocessed Child*

LIFE IS FULL of decisions to make. How many do you think you have already made today? Think about it. Start with when you woke up. (Did you get out of bed to turn off your alarm? That was your first decision—albeit one of the harder ones.) Take a moment and make a mental list of every decision you have made up until the moment you opened this book and started reading. Chances are if you have been up more than a couple of hours, that list has 20, 30, or even more items on it by now. That is because life really is full of decisions—billions of them over the course of a lifetime.

Without a doubt, one of the biggest decisions any person ever makes is whether or not to have a child. Ironically, once that decision has been made and a person transforms into a parent, decisions multiply. Choosing a name is only the beginning—what about bottle feeding versus breastfeeding? Cloth diapers versus disposable? Crib or family bed? Stay-at-home or day care?

One of the most difficult decisions to make as a parent is what kind of education to choose for your children. For the past few generations, the choice was either public or private school. Which was better? In the last 20 years, however, a third choice has grown in popularity: homeschooling. More than two million kids are being taught at home throughout the country today. How did each of these families come to this decision? Like everything else, they learned about it—they read books, met other families, watched shows, listened to speeches, attended workshops—and, more than anything else, they *asked questions*. They asked everyone they could about it who had homeschooled. Why did they do it? Where did they do it? What materials did they use? How did they teach their children? They knew that only through asking questions and learning the answers could they make an informed decision about such an important issue.

This book covers 101 of the most important questions a parent can and should ask about homeschooling. Keep in mind that it is not a replacement for any of those other activities. It is still essential to talk to people, go to presentations, and get information any way you possibly can, but this book can help you get the core facts so you have a working knowledge of homeschooling and know where to go next. These questions address virtually every aspect of teaching your children at home and are intended to give you the head start—the foundation—you need for choosing what is best for your child. That is a decision that every parent wants to make wisely.

Why

AN OLD EXPRESSION says, "Ours is not to question why . . . ," but in this case, it is our duty as parents or guardians to question why with every decision we make. The 11 questions in this section look at some of the key issues in all of home education and will help give you a great beginning as you explore the other sections within the book.

Just for Laughs

Question: What do you call it when a homeschooling mom talks to herself?

Answer: A parent-teacher conference!

---

1. Why do people choose to homeschool?

Why do people take or keep their children out of school? Mostly for three reasons: they think that raising their children is their business not the government's; they enjoy being with their children and watching and helping them learn, and don't want to give that up to others; they want to keep them from being hurt, mentally, physically and spiritually.

—John Holt, *Teach Your Own*

Perhaps no other question in this book is as encompassing—or as complicated—as this one. There is no single, simple answer to it. It is similar to asking people why they chose to get married—or not, or to have children—or not. If you ask 100 different people, you will get 100 different answers. The same is true for home education. If you brought 100 homeschooling families together in one room and asked them why they decided to teach their own children, you would get 100 different responses.

Although the reasons families choose to homeschool that are listed here are the most common, they are not the only ones by a long shot. There are endless variations on these and more that are not listed. In addition, most parents chose to homeschool for a blending of these reasons, not a single one. Again, if you look at the biggest decisions you have made in your life, you most likely did not make them for one sole reason but for a mixture of them.

Reason 1: High-Quality Education

Definitely one of the primary reasons that parents become interested in homeschooling is that they want a high-quality education for their children. Clearly that is the goal of *every* concerned parent, and this book does not mean to imply that only homeschooling parents truly care about their children's education. Instead it encourages all parents to look beyond the norm—public and/or private school—to a third option—homeschooling.

How can parents possibly obtain a better education for their children than the public school system? Here are some of the main ways:

Teacher-to-student ratio

If you have ever been tutored or have tutored someone else, you know how much better it can be to work one-on-one (or one on a couple). Being able to focus on one student means being able to adapt your pace, method, and style to that student's needs. It means staying on the harder concepts until they're learned and speeding past the ones immediately grasped. It means time to ask questions and explore answers. Learning takes less time one-on-one than in a classroom where it is often one-on-20 or more, with time spent taking attendance, collecting and distributing homework, and other daily routines.

Better materials

In homeschooling, you get to choose the materials. You can find them at a variety of places from teacher's supply stores, thrift stores, bookstores, and online. Once again, you can tailor them to your child's needs—if he needs extra help in one subject, you can order more. You will most likely discover that, given time, your child will accelerate in some subjects over another and you can design what you buy based on that, as well as on your child's personal preferences (for example, she loves horses or baseball or any other subject—you can buy that!).

Education to fit the child—instead of the other way around

Schools, whether public or private, are designed—and have been from the very moment the public school system was established—to create conformity. Teaching to large groups of people means expecting them to master the same information at the same pace and the same level just because they happen to be the same age. Children are expected to fit the education and punished (with bad grades, for instance) if they are not able to do so. In homeschooling, the curriculum and education are designed to fit the child. By doing so, he learns at a natural pace instead of an enforced one. Can you remember being forced to read a book and how you felt about it as opposed to reading one of your own choosing? It is often the same with any other material. In homeschooling, if your child learns more easily in the morning, you can do it then—but if she is at her best in the afternoon, wait until then. If your family has an off schedule—working night shifts, or working weekends but not work days—the school hours can be adjusted to fit. Flexibility is one of the biggest advantages to homeschooling.

Dissatisfaction with the public school environment

Many parents are unhappy with the public school system for one reason or another. It may be on principle—they have read about trouble with the school's budget, or a teacher has been fired for inappropriate behavior, or there has been yet another horrific school shooting, or any of a number of things. It may be personal—the parents had a rough time in school, or a neighbor or coworker did, or one of their other children has had issues in school. For one reason or another, the parents are disillusioned with the public school and want something better, or at least different.

Reason 2: Family Cohesiveness

Some families choose to homeschool because they want to maintain family cohesiveness. They hope to avoid anything that splits up the family the way school does. Often these families have been practicing other elements of attachment parenting like extended breastfeeding, family beds, and so on. Just because a child is five or six years old, parents may not feel that it is time for that child to be away from them for hours each day, being taught and influenced by others. Instead, they want to maintain the togetherness they have been enjoying until then. That does not mean they do not want others around, of course. Having friends over, going places, and interacting with people is encouraged but since the parents have already been teaching their children every day, they see no reason for that to change.

School forces families apart in many ways. Parents are often pushed aside for peers and relationships can weaken. For many kids, it just is not cool to like your parents and get along with them. In addition, brothers and sisters who have been playmates for all of their lives are now placed in separate classrooms for hours five days a week. Older children often lose interest in spending time with younger siblings because school encourages the notion that younger means not quite as smart. Instead of the common experiences the siblings had once shared, now they have different teachers, friends, classes, and experiences. Over time, it pushes them apart and divides them in ways that would not have occurred if they had stayed home together. Peers begin to have far more influence over children's behavior than family does—and this can cause problems and concerns.

Reason 3: A Child in Trouble

A number of parents come to homeschooling because they have a child in trouble in some way. This can manifest in several different ways. All of these will be covered in other portions of the book but this gives you an overview.

Bullies

Some children struggle in school every day because of bullying. According to the National Youth Violence Prevention Resource Center, more than 5.7 million kids are involved in bullying, as either the bully, the target, or both.[1] Homeschooling removes this risk—although teasing, bickering, and wrestling are still likely if there are siblings around!

Grades

Failing grades will sometimes motivate parents to try homeschooling. The reasons behind bad grades are numerous but often signal an internal problem with the student. While homeschooling certainly cannot solve all of these problems, it can sometimes alleviate them or at least put some distance between the child and the issue.

ADHD and other learning disabilities

The Centers for Disease Control and Prevention estimate that more than 4.5 million children in the United States today have been diagnosed

---

[1]http://www.safeyouth.org/scripts/faq/bullying.asp

with ADHD, or Attention Deficit Hyperactivity Disorder.[2] The majority of them are boys. Over half of those diagnosed are being given medication such as Ritalin. There are two basic perspectives on ADHD, drugs, and homeschooling: some believe that ADHD is a rare condition that is both misused and overdiagnosed and that homeschooling will take care of most of the symptoms that go with the condition such that medication is not needed. Others believe ADHD is a problem and medication can help, but is better administered and monitored in a homeschooling environment. Many national experts agree with both points of view and you certainly can find families to talk with in either camp.

Special needs

Some families choose to homeschool because their children either are gifted or have some kind of special need. These parents may suspect that the public school system is not able to meet those needs as they had hoped or wanted and believe they can do a better job themselves.

One advantage that homeschooling parents have over all teachers—no matter how skilled—is that they do not just care about their students—they love them. They care about their children's welfare more deeply than any teacher possibly could and this gives them a much deeper interest in meeting whatever needs the children might have. Any type of special need can be adapted to and worked with in the homeschooling situation. Physical problems or challenges can be handled more easily and without the negative labeling that can occur in the public school setting.

Drugs and alcohol use

According to the U.S. Department of Justice's Bureau of Justice Statistics, more than 65% of high school seniors have used alcohol in the last year; more than 43% in the last 30 days. Just under half of the seniors

---

[2]http://www.cdc.gov/ncbddd/adhd/data.html

also used marijuana or other drugs.[3] Homeschooling will certainly not guarantee kids will not use alcohol or drugs—there is no such guarantee—but it does reduce the risk factor substantially. It lowers the access and the influence of peers and gives parents more time to establish a bond that might prevent such risky use.

Reason 4: Religious Beliefs

At the outset of the homeschooling movement, parents were often motivated by a strong desire to merge their children's education with the family's religious beliefs. Indeed, homeschoolers today are still often associated with strong religious belief. Certainly the two are a good mix and this rationale is still prevalent today but a growing number of homeschoolers are doing it entirely for secular reasons.

Reason 5: Educational Beliefs

Some parents choose the homeschooling alternative because they strongly believe that the public school system does not teach the way children learn best. They do not agree that everyone should be taught the same information at the same time, in the same way, at the same pace. They do not want a system that demands conformity rather than supporting individuality. They worry about their children being labeled when they happen to be different in one way or another.

Other Reasons

Besides reasons just discussed, there are dozens of factors that influence the decision in smaller ways, such as:

- more flexible schedule
- sleeping in and staying up late
- no back-to-school wardrobes to purchase

---

[3]http://www.ojp.gov/bjs/dcf/du.htm

- learning about the world right along with the kids
- less hassle for those who choose not to get vaccinations

Reasons why a family may choose to homeschool often change over time. A family may start off doing it for one reason and then, as they gain experience, and both the parents and the children mature, those reasons may evolve. That is normal and expected.

The reasons for homeschooling may differ dramatically from one family to the next, but the bottom line is the same: All homeschooling parents do their utmost to find and make the best educational choices for their children.

Further Resources on This Topic

FAQ about Homeschooling
http://www.holtgws.com/faqabouthomescho.html

Parents' reasons for homeschooling from the National Center for
   Education Statistics
http://nces.ed.gov/pubs2006/homeschool/parentsreasons.asp

2. Why do I need a support group?

Independent, marching to a different drummer, following their hearts and minds people who have chosen to educate their children at home and in the wider world tend toward self-sufficiency. Some people feel they don't need or want to get together with other homeschoolers on a regular basis, but as social beings there is much we can gain from associating with one another. None of us is as smart as all of us.

—Katherine Houk, in Linda Dobson,
The Homeschooling Book of Answers

Initially, you may think: "A support group? Why in the world does a person need one of these?" The truth is, homeschooling can be lonely at first for some people. You're suddenly a member of a new kind of minority.

Sometimes you can feel separated or at odds with your family or friends, especially when you first get started. If they disapprove of what you are doing or, more likely, do not understand it, tension can result.

A support group can help alleviate all of that. In addition, the people in it can provide vital help by answering your questions, listening to your rants, guiding you to good resources, introducing you to new friends, sharing curriculum, making play dates with your kids, carpooling with you to field trips, empathizing with your frustrations, and delighting in your victories.

How do you find a support group? There are a number of ways. Start with these:

- Check homeschooling books and magazines for national and state organizations. They can usually refer you to any support groups in your area.
- Go to teacher supply stores and ask. Check to see if they have a bulletin board. Also check the bulletin boards at grocery stores, natural food stores, food co-ops, libraries, and bookstores.
- Check with area churches.
- Ask any homeschoolers you meet in person or online.
- Ask at your local library for any names.
- Contact your local newspapers and see whether they have done any recent stories on homeschooling. They may have some names to share with you.
- Google *homeschool support groups* along with your city and state.
- Go online to major homeschooling sites and type *support groups* in the search box.
- Check with your local La Leche League.

You might have noticed that we have not suggested contacting your local school system or State Department of Education for homeschooling contacts. That was not an oversight. While there are certainly exceptions to the rule, for the most part, the local schools and DOE are not going to know much about the homeschooling groups and families in their region. Moreover, by contacting them, you open yourself up to the chance that they might try to interfere or stop you from making this educational decision.

If you have trouble finding any support groups in your area, post your own notice on those same bulletin boards. Leave your email address or phone number, whichever you prefer, and ask people to contact you if they are interested in starting a support group or know of one already in operation.

If you simply cannot find a group in your area or if the one you do find does not suit your needs (for example, the children are not the same age as yours, or its religious or secular focus does not match yours), you may want to consider starting your own group. Yes, it will take a lot of effort but in the end it will most likely be very worth it for all the new friends and opportunities it will bring into your life.

Further Resources on This Topic

"Starting a Support Group," A to Z Home's Cool
http://homeschooling.gomilpitas.com/weblinks/supportStart.htm

3. Why should I attend a conference?

I go to conferences like a dry sponge, looking to absorb as much motivation as I can. With four children, there are always trials to go through in our homeschool, and I am interested to hear how others solved their problems and kept their eye on the prize. Like a run-down battery, I need recharging and refocusing, because inevitably, by the end of the school year, I can get a bit hazy about "why" we did this in the first place . . . sometimes just an encouraging talk can clear the fog and remind me of my purpose once more. There is always something new to hear, and even something old that needs to be heard again.[4]

> —Amy Pak, creator of History through the Ages
> historical timeline figures at
> www.homeschoolinthewoods.com

---

[4]http://www.crosswalk.com/homeschool/11603903/page0/)

Simply put, there are three main reasons to attend a homeschooling conference: the things you can learn, the people you can meet, and the products you can buy. A homeschooling conference is a wonderful opportunity to be surrounded by people who are doing the same things you are. Suddenly, you are not in the minority at all. Everywhere you turn you will find other families who have made many of the same choices you have made. A conference can truly be an energizing, renewing, uplifting experience not to be missed.

First, you will learn, learn, learn. Whether held locally, statewide, or even nationally, conferences are full of classes, workshops, panels, and presentations geared to help you be a better homeschooling parent. You will hear ideas, methods, perspectives, opinions, thoughts, and concepts that you had not considered before. You will find out how other homeschooling families teach, work, play, and live.

Next, you will meet other homeschoolers in your city, state, or region. You may discover a future best friend for yourself or for your kids. Hanging out and talking to other people may be the highlight of the entire experience for you. You may even find that you have a homeschooling family living around the corner. You will find people who sympathize and empathize, instruct and inspire, and most of all, listen and understand. You will get the opportunity to see many homeschooling kids of all ages—and be reassured that they do grow up and turn out well. You will likely get the chance to meet some of the authorities in the homeschooling field (they are the keynote speakers and teachers at many conferences) as well.

Finally, you will get the chance to see endless products and services designed especially for homeschoolers, thanks to the many vendors who also attend the conferences. There will be books, curricula, toys, magazines, educational games, and arts and crafts materials. All of it will look tempting so before you go, decide how much you can safely spend and then stick to your budget. Your children will probably find things that they want too, so keep their demands in mind as you figure out your spending limits. Many homeschoolers wait until the end of the conference to make their choices because they will have had more time to mull over which are the best choices for their families.

Speaking of money, homeschooling conferences are not free, so when you find one in your area, you might want to start setting aside money for it. Costs vary widely depending on where it is held, how long it lasts, and who will be speaking, but typical costs include:

- **Entrance Fees.** These can vary depending on whether you are coming alone, with a partner, and/or with kids. Many conferences offer a discounted family rate. The fees also tend to vary depending on the length of the conference; clearly, the longer it is, the more it will cost. If it is held over multiple days, there are often different fees for whatever portion of the conference you are planning to attend, from a single workshop to the entire thing.
- **Hotel Fees.** If your conference is not local such that you can drive to and from it easily, you will likely have hotel costs. Most hotels offer discounts on their rooms for the duration of the conference. Other possibilities to cut costs include camping nearby, sharing a room with another attendee, or connecting with area homeschoolers and asking to stay with them.
- **Food Fees.** Many conferences include the option to order food when you register. Restaurants or caterers might come in to serve meals, or the conference might be held in a venue that includes a restaurant. Ordering your meals through the conference is rarely the most cost-effective choice (a prepacked cooler of PB and Js, applesauce, and juice is certainly less expensive) but it is convenient and gives you less to tote around.
- **Extra Fees.** Additional fees may be added for things like state support group membership, materials fees for some craft classes, and the like. Be sure to check the registration form for an early bird discount, which applies if you turn in the form before the deadline. Also consider taking out a membership in the organization sponsoring the event. The membership cost is frequently offset by the discount you get when you register. Membership often includes other perks as well, so this can be a wise choice.

This may sound like a lot of money—and it can add up to more than $100. However, most families walk away at the end of the conference feeling that the money was well worth what they gained from the experience. A homeschooling conference can reenergize you, persuade a reluctant spouse, excite kids, and give you all a sense of direction you might not yet have found. It is worth every penny, so start saving now.

Conferences are not the only activities you can attend related to homeschooling. Do some research and you can also find, depending on where you live, camp-outs, retreats, and curricula swaps and fairs. There are even homeschooling Disney trips and cruises!

Further Resources on This Topic

"An Insider's Guide to Homeschool Conventions," by Maggie Hogan
http://www.crosswalk.com/homeschool/11603903/

"Ten Timeless Tips for Tackling a Homeschool Convention"
http://heartofthematteronline.com/ten-timeless-tips-for-tackling-a
   -homeschool-convention

For a nationwide list of homeschooling conferences, visit
http://homeschooling.gomilpitas.com/calendar/events.htm

4. Why are there so many different styles of homeschooling?

From the beginning I taught my kids to have good character and to have a good work ethic; the rest will take care of itself. After so many years, I have found it to be true.

         —Dawn, homeschooling mom

The answer to this question is an easy one: There are so many different styles of homeschooling because there are so many different styles of families and children. The key to home education is that it refuses to subscribe to the philosophy that one size fits all. Because of this, a number of different approaches to homeschooling exist. They are all listed here with brief descriptions, but will be explained in greater depth in the *What* section of this book.

Choosing a style of homeschooling right when you are beginning is a little like picking out what car you want to drive when you are ten years old. You really do not have the wisdom and experience to make a good choice. As you look over the following styles of homeschooling, keep these very important keys in mind.

- Whatever style you start with, it is almost guaranteed not to be the one you will stay with. You will evolve, as will your children, and in the process your style of homeschooling will shift, sometimes in small ways and sometimes dramatically. It is a trial-and-error process. Ways to recognize that the style you are using is not the right one include growing frustration on your part or your children's, a constant reluctance to homeschool, or repeated disagreements and conflict over working together.
- A style that works for you may not work well for your children. This is something you will have to work out carefully. Whose preference is more important to you? You, as the teacher, or your children, as the students?
- Most families blend styles rather than sticking with just one.
- If one style of homeschooling fits one of your children perfectly, it most likely will not fit another child. Kids have different learning styles, attitudes, abilities, and personalities. Remember that one size does *not* fit all, so be prepared to be flexible depending on which child you're working with.

Here is a quick overview of the most common styles of homeschooling.

Traditional/School at Home

For most newcomers to homeschooling, this is the method that feels the most comfortable. It is modeled after the public school, from grades and report cards to record keeping and strict hours. It is basically the same as school, except in a different environment and with a different teacher. For most parents, this is what is most familiar and what constitutes *school*. It is very teacher-centered and teacher-led. However, this is the most expensive method (families typically buy prepackaged curricula for a specific grade level) and it is also the one with the highest risk of complete burnout, since it demands so much of a parent.

Unit Studies

This style is based more on your child's interests. Whatever topic he or she is interested in is foundation for the unit and the parents find a way to incorporate the core subjects (math, spelling, science, art, and history) into it. For example, if your daughter loves horses, you can develop a unit that measures the height and speed of horses (math), write a story about a favorite horse (spelling, English skills), read about how horses have played a pivotal role in the development of the country (history), draw pictures of horses (art), and study the physiology of horse muscles to understand how they are capable of such hard work (science). Parents typically create their own curricula from a variety of resources.

Classical

The classical method has been utilized by some of the greatest minds in history and dates all the way back to the Middle Ages. It is based on a different set of skills: grammar, logic, and rhetoric. The focus is on critical thinking skills and is done in stages, based on a child's age and abilities.

Eclectic

If you have ever prepared a dish for dinner that is made up of a little of this and a little of that, you already know the philosophy behind this style of home education. Another name for this style is simply *relaxed homeschooling*. It is a mixture of whatever works for your family and typically develops over time and a lot of trial and error.

Unschooling

If school at home is on one end of the homeschooling spectrum, unschooling is on the opposite one. Instead of being teacher-centered, it is child-centered. People who are new to the idea of homeschooling often struggle with this style because it is so different from the public school model most are accustomed to. Unschooling relies on life as curriculum, and usually follows the child's interest for all activities. People who do not understand the philosophy may perceive children as not doing anything all day—but that is simply because these kids are often learning information in their own way, not with a workbook or a lesson.

Religious Based

This is the style that has been most closely associated with home-schooling. When homeschooling first started, many of the families who chose to do it were motivated by religious reasons, wanting to blend their children's educational and spiritual training. In this style of homeschooling, curricula for most if not all topics are tied to the family's religious beliefs and everything is taught from a faith-based perspective. Although Christian homeschooling represents the largest segment, a number of other faiths also incorporate their belief system into their homeschooling.

Internet/Virtual

Perhaps the most modern of methods, this style centers on the use of the Internet via virtual tutors and schools, online curricula, and websites. Some courses are free to use; others have a fee to subscribe. Often referred to as *distance learning* or *correspondence school*, this style is for independent learners who knows their way around the World Wide Web.

As you reviewed these different styles, you might initially have gravitated toward one or the other. You might also immediately have recognized one style fitting as your child more than another one. Those feelings are clues as to where to start, but keep in mind that you are certain to change your mind a number of times along the way. Your first year of homeschooling is often considered a nonstop trial-and-error period, so prepare yourself for it and you just might enjoy the process as you learn more about how you and your children teach and learn.

Further Resources on This Topic

"Homeschooling Approaches"
http://www.homeschool.com/Approaches/

"Methods and Styles Directory"
http://homeschooling.gomilpitas.com/methods/Methods.htm

5. *Why do some families homeschool one child but not another?*

One of the wonderful things about choosing this path is the opportunity for deeper connections among family members. Although they are eight years apart in age, my children have a close relationship. They are both involved in lots of classes and activities, but they run into each other a lot more throughout the week than they would if one was in high school, and the other in elementary school. They also know my husband and me as a real people in a way that we never knew our parents. Over the years, this has become one of my motivations for homeschooling.

—Allyson, homeschooling mom

This is a good question; most likely every family you ask would have a different response to it. What it comes down to, however, is that different children often have different educational needs. While one child may be thriving in the public school system, another may be struggling. One may love going to school, while another dreads it. The decision to homeschool the child who is having difficulty just makes sense.

If you go this route, however, be prepared for the fact that the child who stays in public school may end up rather jealous or resentful of the homeschooled sibling. Being able to sleep in, skip riding the bus, and not deal with school lunches may start looking pretty good. If this happens, give some thought to homeschooling all of your children. Just because a child is doing well in school does not mean he or she would not benefit from homeschooling. Often this child will thrive even more in the home setting. This issue will be discussed in detail in later sections.

6. Why does the idea of homeschooling upset some people so much?

Why do we hate (or at least distrust) these people so much? Methinks American middle-class people are uncomfortable around the home schooled for the same reason the alcoholic is uneasy around the teetotaler. Their very existence represents a rejection of our values, and an indictment of our lifestyles. Those families are willing to render unto Caesar the things that Caesar's be, but they draw the line at their children. Those of us who have put our trust in the secular state (and effectively surrendered our children to it) recognize this act of defiance as a rejection of our values, and we reject them in return.

—Sonny Scott, "Homeschoolers Threaten Our Cultural Comfort," in *Northeast Mississippi Daily Journal*

As you go about homeschooling your kids, many of the people you encounter will be curious about what you do. Some will be interested and want to know more. Some will be baffled and walk away shaking their heads. Still others will be supportive, often saying things like, "Well, I could never do it, but good for you!" There may be a few people, however, who respond to you with hostility or anger. Why? Why should your personal educational choices for your kids upset other people? There are several reasons.

Reason 1: A Reflection on Their Choices
Many people feel that by choosing not to put your children in public school, you are insulting or passing judgment on them because they did. Somehow your decision about your kids makes them feel threatened or rebuffed for making a different choice for theirs. Of course, that is not true—what you are doing does not, in any way, reflect on their choices. But if they feel defensive—and they often do—they may respond negatively to you.

Reason 2: A Reflection on Their Careers
If the person you happen to be talking to works within the public education field (teacher, administrator, school board, and so on),

they may be personally offended because they will see your decision as an indirect statement about their job performance. Once again, you are not insulting their teaching ability or their school policies; you are simply stating that that system is not what you choose for your family.

Reason 3: They Believe the Myths

The myths that surround homeschooling (covered in detail later in this book) are quite pervasive and frequently sway people's opinions. Some people may truly believe that you are damaging your children socially or academically. In their perspective, you are committing a type of child abuse that your child may have to pay for in many different ways. Those with this attitude are usually the most ignorant of what homeschooling actually is, but educating them is not your responsibility.

Reason 4: They Care about Your Children and Are Worried for Their Well-Being

Hard as it may be to believe, some of the people who are bothered the most by homeschooling are the ones who honestly care about your children—such as neighbors, relatives, former teachers, and friends. Because they do not truly understand what homeschooling is and how it works, their concern comes across as anger.

How do you handle people who are negative about your decision? If they are strangers, let it go. Walk away. If they are important to you, however, or if it is clear that the motivation behind their reactions is genuine concern, take the time to rectify the situation. Share a book or article, welcome questions, or arrange a time to have a talk so that they can better understand what you are doing and how it is not any kind of reflection on them. Pat Montgomery, retired president and founder of Clonlara Home-Based Education in Ann Arbor, Michigan, writes, "When a person who questions homeschooling is sincere in her questioning, and open to learning more about the issue, a parent does well to assist her. When the questioner is a faultfinder, lacking an open mind on the subject and only interested in discrediting it, the less said the better."

Further Resources on This Topic

"Overview of Common Arguments against Homeschooling"
http://socyberty.com/education/overview-of-common-arguments
   -against-homeschooling/

"Dealing with Opposition to Homeschooling"
http://www.naturemoms.com/opposition-to-homeschool.html

7. Why do some children want to be homeschooled?

When we first started homeschooling, the advice that got me through the yearly panic attacks was from my husband, "First, do no harm." Since my children had been to public school, we could see how endless questions (What does "realistic" mean on page 32?) turned them off books, how the dull worksheets turned them off math, and how the bullies made them anxious and afraid. My children loved reading and learning, and were surrounded by people who loved and accepted them. That was enough.

—Stephanie, homeschooling mom

Although it seems that most of the time the decision to homeschool lies with the parents, there are situations in which it is the child that comes home and asks to be homeschooled. Why? There are a number of reasons. Children may

- be struggling academically
- feel pressured to use drugs or alcohol
- be being bullied or threatened
- feel they do not fit in with their classmates
- feel they are being pushed to engage in illegal behavior
- think they are being treated unfairly by a teacher
- be bored in the classroom
- be left behind or held back
- be learning faster than the rest of the class
- be feeling lonely in the school environment

- be having trouble learning at the class pace
- be feeling incongruent with the school's learning styles
- be dealing with a learning disability
- need more physical/mental stimulation
- have discipline problems

Any of these reasons—or any others that children may come to you with—are valid enough at least to warrant a discussion about homeschooling. Certainly some of the complaints might be temporary, and a day or two later, your child is not remotely interested in being homeschooled. Still, the request should be given both time and respect regardless.

Further Resources on This Topic

"How Do I Convince My Parents to Homeschool Me?"
http://www.purehomeschooling.com/2009/05/how-do-i-convince
-my-parents-to.html

8. Why do people quit homeschooling?

Frequently, parents new to homeschooling will feel overwhelmed and panicked at the thought of trying to figure out how to educate their children at home. I always recommend taking it one year at a time, and only continue as long as it is working for everyone in the family. Our family has enjoyed eleven years so far, and it still works best for us.

—Allyson, homeschooling mom

Why do people who have made the commitment to homeschool stop? There are a number of reasons.

Reason 1: The Child Wants to Go to School
Sometimes homeschooling comes to an end because the child sincerely wants to go to or return to school. While this request should be honored and considered, keep in mind the child's age and reasons. Very

young children may not yet have the maturity and wisdom to make a serious decision like this. Their reasons may not be serious either. For example, a younger child might want to go to school so that he can get new school supplies or she can get a back to school wardrobe. An older child might want to spend more time with friends or join the school's sports team. All of those things can be accomplished without going back to school. Knowing that and knowing how to achieve it may satisfy your children's request without setting foot inside the school.

Reason 2: The Parents Burn Out

It is not unusual for parents, especially those in the first year of homeschooling, to burn out and not want to do it anymore. Typically, burning out is an indication that you have taken on more than you can handle—not difficult to do if you are carrying the roles of parent, employee, spouse, and teacher.

Burnout can be prevented—and if it has already happened, it can be treated without putting an end to homeschooling. The key to all of it is pinpointing where your stress is coming from. Do you have too much responsibility weighing on you? Delegate it. Have your kids take over some household chores. Ask your spouse to help with some of the teaching. Hire a housecleaner or gardener, if you can. Share teaching responsibilities with other homeschooling families. Exchange childcare with other parents so you can have some time off. Personal time for yourself to pursue your own interests and recharge is a must in order to avoid burning out.

Are you committing yourself to too much outside the house? Are there activities or obligations that you can postpone until a period in life where you have more free time? This is a time where you can be selfish with your time and have the freedom to say *no* when asked to serve on a committee or volunteer for a good cause, and to other invitations.

Many times the main source of the stress is homeschooling itself. Chances are, if you are trying to do school at home, you are overworked and overwhelmed. It is the most demanding of all techniques and can wear out many parents. Rather than give up on homeschooling altogether, however, why not try adopting a more relaxed approach to teaching, at least temporarily? It might give you the break you need, plus give you time to experiment with a less demanding method.

Reason 3: The Kids Get Older

Some homeschooling families decide to stop homeschooling when their children are ready to enter junior high or high school. Subjects get harder at this level, and the idea of teaching a subject you do not really know or know well can be quite intimidating. It is possible, however, and there are a number of ways to achieve it, all of which will be outlined in another part of this book. Suffice to say, however, that just because your children are getting older and learning more complex material is not a reason to quit homeschooling. It is a bump in the road, not a stop sign.

Reason 4: Both Parents Need to Go to Work Full Time

When both parents have to work full time in order to make ends meet in a family, then homeschooling may have to temporarily stop—or maybe not. There are other options that can be (and will be, further on in this book) explored—including working split shifts, getting help from grandparents and others, independent curricula, and more.

The reasons people choose to quit homeschooling are often just as valid and take just as much time and thought as the decision to homeschool did. It may be the right decision for your family—but it should be taken seriously and alternatives explored to avoid giving up too soon.

Further Resources on This Topic

"Avoiding Homeschool Burnout," by Isabel Shaw
http://school.familyeducation.com/home-schooling/stress/38363.html

"Homeschool Burnout: How to Recognize and Avoid the Signs of Burnout," by Christine Alcott
http://homeschooling.suite101.com/article.cfm/homeschool_burnout

9. Why should I talk to a number of families before making the decision to homeschool?

Every family has its own micro-culture. We have a language, shared ethics, a collective sense of humor, a belief system and a history of shared experiences. When we're learning within our micro-culture, things make sense in profound way and we have a deeper appreciation for other cultures.

—Brandy, homeschooling mom

As you have already read, homeschooling is a big decision that truly requires a lot of groundwork. While reading books is extremely important, nothing is as helpful as seeing homeschooling in practice. One of the best ways to understand any of the methods or perspectives explained here is to see them being used in a family. Meeting and talking with as many homeschooling families as possible will give you that chance.

How do you find families? Remember that search you did for local and state homeschooling organizations and support groups? It is time to put that information to work for you. Make some calls and contact these people. Ask if there are some parents you could talk to on the telephone to ask questions (and have your questions written down before you call!). Ask if you can arrange a play date for your kids. Offer to meet at a local park on a sunny afternoon or in a nearby coffee house on a rainy morning.

Find a support group in your area and attend a meeting. Go with your list of questions and just let everyone know you are considering homeschooling and would like to find out more. Almost certainly you will be warmly welcomed and parents will be more than happy to share their thoughts, advice, and encouragement with you. Take the time to observe the children while you are there. Seeing how normal and happy they are can often put your mind at ease right away about homeschooling.

The more information you have, the better decision you can make. Talking to actual homeschoolers gives you the chance to ask questions and match real situations with ideas from books.

Further Resources on This Topic

Homeschool World Forum
http://www.home-school.com/forums/

Homeschool Spot
www.homeschoolspot.com

A to Z Home's Cool Chat Room
http://homeschooling.gomilpitas.com/extras/A2Zchat.htm#

10. Why should I register with the state—or why should I not?

Don't worry. When you trust your children, you eventually all settle into a place of comfortable self-assurance.
　　　　　—Lilian Jones, *The Homeschooling Book of Answers*

The legalities of homeschooling will be covered in depth in another part of this book. Some states require you to register with the state's department of education. Typically, a registration form simply asks you to supply the name and age of each of your school-age children and what kind of curriculum you will be using to teach language arts, social science, mathematics, fine arts, biological and physical sciences, and PE and health (depending on the age of the kids).

Do all families living in states requiring registration choose to comply? No. In fact, some experts believe that fewer than a third of them comply (which is why numbers coming from a state's DOE are often considered extremely unreliable). Why do they do this? They simply do not want the DOE knowing about them because they do not want that organization to interfere with them in any way. These families want to be left alone to raise and teach their children without input or influence of the public school system and many believe that the only way to ensure that is not to let the DOE know they exist.

What happens if you do not register? It depends on the state; usually absolutely nothing other than another request to register.

So: should you register if it is a requirement within your state? If you want to ensure that you are following your homeschooling law to the letter, yes, you should. If you are not sure you want to, talk to other homeschoolers and get their perspectives on it. Again, the only wise decision is the informed one, so find out the details and then make a choice.

Further Resources on This Topic

A typical state registration form can be seen at http://www.isbe.net/research/pdfs/hs_registration.pdf

11. Why is homeschooling growing steadily?

I'd rather my kids grow from the inside out, instead of the outside in.
—Karen, homeschooling mom

Twenty years ago, homeschoolers were an oddity. Tell someone you were homeschooling and they automatically assumed that something was wrong with your children—or with you. Today the more common response is, "Oh! My sister-in-law/brother/cousin/coworker/neighbor is doing that too." Homeschooling has grown steadily and the media is covering this trend. For example, *USA Today* published a story (January 5, 2009) by Janice Lloyd titled "Home Schooling Grows." In it, she wrote, "The ranks of America's home-schooled children have continued a steady climb over the past five years, and new research suggests broader reasons for the appeal."[5]

The reasons families choose to homeschool are listed in great detail earlier in this book, but as the years have passed, those reasons have changed and expanded. For example, in the latest survey of homeschoolers (2007), a new category asked about families who choose to home educate because of an interest in nontraditional approaches. The

---

[5]http://www.usatoday.com/news/education/2009-01-04-homeschooling_N.htm

survey also showed that parents are deciding to homeschool to save money and to increase family time.

In recent years, another reason for the increase has—unfortunately—been a desire to keep children safe. Ever since the 1999 school shooting at Denver's Columbine High School, children's safety has been a growing concern. Other incidents, such as the shooting at an Amish schoolhouse in 2006 and the Virginia Tech incident in 2007, have only reinforced those fears.

With the recession of 2009, a growing number of families have also chosen homeschooling in the hopes that it will cost less (and for the most part, it does). This and other reasons have combined to keep homeschooling a strong educational choice throughout the country.

Further Resources on This Topic

"Trends and Growth in Homeschooling," by Karrie Emms
http://homeschooling.suite101.com/article.cfm/trends_and_growth_
   in_homeschooling

"Homeschool Statistics: Data on Homeschooling"
http://www.time4learning.com/homeschool/homeschoolstatistics.shtml

Who

IN THIS SECTION, you will meet some of the biggest names in the homeschooling movement, as well as hear about the roles people play when home educating.

Just for Laughs

Question: How does a homeschooler change a light bulb?

Answer: First, mom checks out three books on electricity from the library, then the kids make models of light bulbs, read a biography of Thomas Edison, and do a skit based on his life.

Next, everyone studies the history of lighting methods, wrapping up with dipping their own candles.

Then, everyone takes a trip to the store where they compare types of light bulbs as well as prices and figure out how much change they will get if they buy two bulbs for $1.99 and pay with a five-dollar bill.

On the way home, a discussion develops over the history of money and also Abraham Lincoln, as his picture is on the $5 bill.

Finally, after the kids build a homemade ladder out of branches dragged from the woods, mom installs the light bulb.

And there is light!

12. Who are the homeschooling experts?

Trust in your children. They learned how to love, smile, crawl, walk, talk, run, dress themselves, and understand their world before starting school, and they will continue to grow and learn through homeschooling.

> —"The Ten Most Important Things You
> Need to Know about Homeschooling," at
> www.homeschool.com

Today there are many voices speaking out for and about the subject of homeschooling. The shelves at major bookstores carry multiple titles on the subject. This was not always the case, however. The people listed here are some of the pioneering voices in homeschooling then and now.

John Holt

I have used the words "home schooling" to describe the process by which children grow and learn in the world without going, or going very much, to schools, because those words are familiar and quickly understood. But in one very important sense they are misleading. What is most important and valuable about the home as a base for children's growth in the world is not that it is a better school than the schools but that it is not a school at all.

> —John Holt, *Teach Your Own*

John Holt (1923–1985) is often referred to as the "father" of homeschooling. Without a doubt, it was his words that first inspired a generation of readers to see education in an entirely different light. His
books, *How Children Fail* (1964) and *How Children Learn* (1967), led
to his becoming a speaker for school reform. Finally, he decided that
schools were beyond redemption and became an ardent advocate of
alternative education. In 1977, he started the first homeschooling magazine, *Growing without Schooling*, and four years later, his primary
book on homeschooling, *Teach Your Own*, was published.

Patrick Farenga

Homeschooling is not just another instruction-delivery system; it
shows us alternative ways to teach and learn, and to participate in
family and community life; ways to find work or get into higher edu-
cation without jumping through the standardized hoops of mass-
market schooling; ways to use school rather than have school use you.
　　　　　　　　　　　　　—Patrick Farenga, *Teach Your Own*

Patrick Farenga was a personal friend and colleague of John Holt, and
after Holt's death Farenga took the helm of Holt Associates Inc. A
homeschooling father of three, he has written numerous articles and is
author of *The Beginner's Guide to Homeschooling*. He has appeared frequently at homeschool conferences and on national television and
radio shows such as the *Today Show*, NPR's the *Merrow Report*, and
CNN's *Parenting Today*. He now works as an educational consultant for
parents who want to find out more about homeschooling and
unschooling.

To find out more, check out www.patfarenga.com.

Grace Llewellyn

Your teacher cannot bridge the gap between what you know and
what you want to know. For his words to "educate" you, you must
welcome them, think about them, find somewhere for your mind to
organize them, and remember them. Your learning is your job, not
your teacher's job. And all you need to start with is desire. You do not

*need a schoolteacher to get knowledge—you can get it from looking
at the world, from watching films, from conversations, from reading,
from asking questions, from experience.*

—Grace Llewellyn, *The Teenage Liberation Handbook*[1]

Known as an *unschooling advocate*, Grace Llewellyn has written several books including *The Teenage Liberation Handbook and Real Lives: Eleven Teenagers Who Don't Go to School.* She also co-authored *Guerilla Learning: How to Get Your Kids a Real Education with or without School* with Amy Silver. For the last 14 years, she has hosted Not Back to School Camp, a camp for homeschooled teenagers. Two sessions are held in Oregon, while a third is held in West Virginia. Each session hosts more than 100 teens from all over the country who come to hang out, talk, laugh, and discover with others like themselves.

To find out more, check out: http://nbtsc.org/.

Raymond and Dorothy Moore

*Remember, we do not say that all home teaching is perfect, but we
do warn those parents who try to teach as they were taught in conventional schools: From fifty years of research and long experience
with unnumbered home teachers, we are not certain that they will
work harder, worry more and accomplish less. . . . Parents involved
in mass education can also learn much from homeschooling—the
greatest educational method ever invented.*

—Raymond and Dorothy Moore,
The Successful Homeschool Family Handbook

Sometimes referred to as the grandparents of homeschooling, Raymond and Dorothy Moore were involved in helping and supporting homeschoolers for more than 50 years. They are the creators of the

---

[1]http://selfmadescholar.com/b/2009/04/07/great-thinkers-on-self-education
-grace-llewellyn/

Moore Formula, a three-part educational philosophy based on study, manual work/entrepreneurship, and home and/or community service. The Moores were also known for their strong belief in *delayed academics,* according to which no formal education of any kind is started until the child is between eight and ten years old. Their research was published in their 1972 book, *Better Late than Early.*

To find out more, check out http://www.moorehomeschooling.com/article.php?id=9.

Linda Dobson

Homeschooling is a grassroots educational alternative that originates with the seed of parental love and commitment and blossoms into a lush garden of personal empowerment for child and parent.
—Linda Dobson, *The Homeschooling Book of Answers*

Linda Dobson is a longtime advocate of homeschooling. As a regular columnist in *Home Education Magazine* and the author of books like *The Art of Education* and *The Homeschooling Book of Answers,* she was also one of the first writers to place an article about home education in a mainstream magazine (*Good Housekeeping*).

To find out more, check out http://homeschoolcronescafe.ning.com/.

Mark and Helen Hegener

We've always liked this analogy (homeschoolers as pioneers) as the pioneers had to be brave and courageous and confident souls, working together, supporting each other, blazing new trails, building foundations for those who would come later. Because those scared but courageous homeschool pioneers forged ahead, parents now have a wealth of support to draw from, but important questions still face us on the trail ahead. And the questions are changing even as we're finding answers. Homeschooling is changing, evolving and developing and the decisions you make for your family—the ways in which you choose to help your children learn—are part and parcel of the change.
—Tamra B. Orr, *Asking Questions, Finding Answers*

The Hegeners unschooled their own five children and have gone on to support the concept through their publication, *Home Education Magazine*, since 1983. One of the rare secular homeschooling publications, HEM also publishes books pertinent to home education. Today, the Hegeners are still publishing the magazine and watching as their grandchildren are homeschooled as well.

To find out more, check out www.homeedmag.com.

David and Micki Colfax

The answer to your question is, we did as little as possible and we did as much as possible [with our children]. I think that most people are uncomfortable with that kind of answer. It sounds like a statement in which we are trying to be evasive, but that is really at the heart of it. That is one of the things that we try to convey to parents in our very short conversations with them. If you come into homeschooling with an ideology of education that is fully fleshed out, I think you are going to have some very serious problems at some point in your later educational endeavors.[2]

—David Colfax

In the late 1980s, the Colfaxes brought homeschooling to the media forefront when their three homeschooled sons went on to be accepted at Harvard. It was one of the first validations that yes, homeschooled kids can go to college—even the most prestigious Ivy League ones—and do well. Raised on a ranch where they had built their house, and raised sheep, goats, and other animals, the Colfax family focused on reading novels and fiction. "Our schedules were very unstructured," recalls their son, Reed. "Some days we did a lot of homework, some days we had none. It depended on the weather and what had to be done on the ranch." The family wrote the books *Homeschooling for Excellence* and *Hard Times in Paradise*. All three sons graduated from Harvard and have gone into the fields of medicine, law, and culinary arts.

---

[2]http://www.homeschoolnewslink.com/homeschool/articles/vol7iss1/vol7iss1_ColfaxInterview.shtml

John Taylor Gatto

I do not think we'll get rid of schools any time soon, certainly not in my lifetime, but if we're going to change what's rapidly becoming a disaster of ignorance, we need to realize that the school institution "schools" very well, though it does not "educate"; that's inherent in the design of the thing. It's not the fault of bad teachers or too little money spent. It's just impossible for education and schooling ever to be the same thing.

—John Taylor Gatto

In 1991, after having won the New York State Teacher of the Year award (three times!), John Taylor Gatto surprised everyone by quitting via the Op Ed page of the *Wall Street Journal*, stating that he no longer wanted to harm children. He became a popular speaker and an advocate of educational alternatives such as homeschooling and is author of a number of books, including *Dumbing Us Down: The Hidden Curriculum of Compulsory Schooling*, *The Exhausted School*, and *The Underground History of American Education*. His presentations give parents an inside look at what is happening in the public school system and inspire many to choose a different route for their children.

To find out more, check out www.johntaylorgatto.com.

13. Who started the homeschooling movement?

We who believe that children want to learn about the world, are good at it, and can be trusted to do it with very little adult coercion or interference, are probably no more than one percent of the population, if that. And we are not likely to become the majority in my lifetime. This doesn't trouble me much anymore, as long as this minority keeps on growing.

—John Holt, *Teach Your Own*

A partial answer to that question can be found somewhere in the middle of all of the names in the previous question. All of the people listed were integral forces in helping families all over the world learn about a viable educational alternative. They spoke up and spoke out. They wrote for newspapers, newsletters, magazines, and books. They shared what they had learned and what they questioned.

The other part of the answer is that parents—families just like you— started and maintained the homeschooling movement. Their efforts to find the best education for their children—their passion, dedication, and determination—helped start a change and keep it going.

Further Resources on This Topic

The history of homeschooling

http://homeschooling.gomilpitas.com/weblinks/historyHS.htm

http://homeschooling.suite101.com/article.cfm/modern_homeschool
  _movement

http://www.synergyfield.com/history.asp

14. Who does the teaching in the family?

That depends on you and your family. It is important that you keep reminding yourself that in homeschooling, *no one size fits all*. How you teach, what you teach, and who teaches it is *completely up to you*. That can sound intimidating but it is also very freeing. It opens up virtually limitless possibilities. In your house, the teaching can be done by

- you
- your partner
- your other children
- outside teachers
- tutors
- online classes and teachers
- textbooks
- DVDs and films
- CDs
- magazines and newspapers

- the Internet
- friends
- neighbors
- coworkers
- community college classes
- satellite high school classes
- churches

Most of the teaching will be done by you and/or your partner, of course, but it does not have to be limited to that, by any means. You can bring in outside teachers and mentors of all kinds to teach topics you do not know well or need more advanced help with. You can enroll your kids in all kinds of classes, homeschooling-based or otherwise.

Who does the teaching depends on your daily schedules. It also depends on your personal strengths. Maybe one of you excels at teaching, or is more proficient in science, or is more comfortable with hands-on experiments and field trips, or with workbooks and reading aloud. As with everything else, figuring out who teaches what is part of the trial-and-error process.

Do not overlook one other source of teaching—the children themselves. Many homeschoolers evolve into independent learners (*autodidacts*). They specialize in teaching themselves. As a parent, it is your job to make sure your kids have access to whatever materials they need. For more on this concept, check out *I Learn Better by Teaching Myself*, by Agnes Leistico.

Further Resources on This Topic

How to work and homeschool
http://www.homeschoolviews.com/feature/homeschooldad.html

Homeschool dads
http://homeschooling.gomilpitas.com/weblinks/dads.htm
www.homeschooldads.com

15. Who can act as a mentor/tutor/helper with my children?

Life is an ongoing learning process not limited to age or place. Our world is full of people who know so much that we do not know! If we keep our minds open we can learn something different from each person we meet. Our children can do the same, especially if we do not narrow the definition of learning to just the standard school subjects.
—Donn and Jean Reed, in Linda Dobson,
The Homeschooling Book of Answers

Again, that depends on you and your family. Virtually anyone in your life can be a mentor or tutor to your children. The choices are unlimited.

Make a list of the people you know—friends, family, coworkers, neighbors, church members, personal mentors, and so on. Next to their names, write some of their skills. Be sure you think beyond the standard academic subjects. Do you have a cousin who is a great artist? How about a colleague who is an expert tennis player? Do you live next door to a woman who knows how to grow gorgeous roses or to a man who does amazing wood carvings? Does your older brother actually enjoy calculus or does your sister-in-law know how to speak French fluently? All of these are potential mentors or tutors for your children.

Further Resources on This Topic

"The Value of a Mentor," by Katharine Hansen, PhD
http://www.quintcareers.com/mentor_value.html

"Finding a Mentor for Your Gifted Child," by Lorel Shea
http://www.bellaonline.com/articles/art42217.asp

16. Who is being homeschooled in the United States?

As homeschoolers who want our friends and relatives, the general public, legislators, and others to have accurate and meaningful information about homeschooling, we realize that we must take responsibility for providing it. However, using the results of a recent survey of homeschoolers will not only provide inaccurate and misleading information but will also limit our homeschooling options and decrease our freedoms.

—Larry and Susan Kaseman, "Survey and Lobbyists Cause Problems for Homeschoolers," in *Home Education Magazine*

Families who are exploring the possibility of homeschooling often look for numbers and statistics to point out how many children are being taught at home, how well they are doing on national tests, how many are being admitted into colleges and universities, and other such statistics. Some of these numbers do exist but how reliable or accurate they are is often brought into question. Why? There are a number of reasons.

First of all, the majority of homeschoolers do not have any interest in participating in surveys, especially those conducted by the government or the Department of Education. Homeschoolers do not want interference of any kind and tend to stay quiet and unobtrusive if at all possible. The ones that do tend to participate in surveys are not a true representation of the average homeschooler. A survey showing the number of homeschoolers, for example, is often based on the number of *registered* homeschoolers—and that is only a fraction of them. When the December 2008 report, "1.5 Million Homeschooled Students in the United States in 2007," from the National Center for Education Statistics[3] reported their numbers, were they accurate? Probably not. The number is most likely much higher.

Secondly, the surveys tend to be based on a public school model. For example, they will show how homeschoolers performed on national tests—even though national tests are not geared in the least for how homeschooling families teach. When homeschoolers do take these

---

[3]http://nces.ed.gov/pubs2009/2009030.pdf

national tests, they almost always tend to rank as high as, if not higher than, their public school counterparts. However, how significant is that? Susannah Sheffer, author of *Writing Because We Love To: Homeschoolers at Work* and *A Sense of Self: Listening to Homeschooled Adolescent Girls*, writes,

> *I could answer this question by telling you how well homeschoolers generally score on standardized tests and about the research studies that compare homeschoolers' test scores with scores of other students. But I do not think these facts get at what's most interesting or most important about homeschoolers or their academic experience. What distinguishes homeschoolers, in my mind, is not just their often impressive skill and accomplishment, but their attitude toward their work, their reasons for doing what they do.*

Despite the fact that national standardized tests do not really show what students know and do not address how or what homeschooled students learn, and regardless of the fact that the student may have been homeschooled for a week or for an entire lifetime—despite all this, people still want to see the numbers. So, here they are—inaccurate though they might be: According to makers of the ACT, the average homeschoolers ACT score in 2009 was 22.5, higher than the national average of 21.1 (on a scale of 1–36).[4]

Further Resources on This Topic

SAT and other college entrance tests
http://homeschooling.gomilpitas.com/olderkids/CollegeTests.htm

"Home-Schooled Kids Defy Stereotypes, Ace SAT Test," by Daniel Golden, *Wall Street Journal*
http://www.oakmeadow.com/resources/articles/WSJArticle.htm

---

[4]http:/hslda.org/docs/media/2009/200908270.asp

17. Who has been homeschooled in the past (well-known homeschoolers)?

One look at all of the famous names on these lists may be enough to sway the most reluctant parent. Here are just a few of the people who have influenced history—and were educated at home.

PRESIDENTS

John Adams
John Quincy Adams
Grover Cleveland
James Garfield
William Henry Harrison
Andrew Jackson
Thomas Jefferson
Abraham Lincoln
James Madison
Franklin Delano Roosevelt
Theodore Roosevelt
John Tyler
George Washington
Woodrow Wilson

INVENTORS

Alexander Graham Bell
Leonardo da Vinci
Thomas Edison
Benjamin Franklin
Guglielmo Marconi
Eli Whitney
Orville and Wilbur Wright

COMPOSERS

Irving Berlin
Noel Coward
Felix Mendelssohn
Wolfgang Amadeus Mozart
John Philip Sousa

WRITERS

Hans Christian Andersen
Margaret Atwood
Pearl S. Buck
Willa Cather
Agatha Christie
Samuel Clemens/Mark Twain
Charles Dickens
Robert Frost
Alex Haley
L. Ron Hubbard
C.S. Lewis
Christopher Paolini
Beatrix Potter
Carl Sandburg
George Bernard Shaw
Laura Ingalls Wilder
Walt Whitman

CELEBRITIES

Christina Aguilera	Jennifer Love Hewitt
Alan Alda	Lindsay Lohan
Louis Armstrong	Frankie Muniz
Charlie Chaplin	Hayden Panettiere
Hilary Duff	LeAnn Rimes
Dakota Fanning	Jordin Sparks
Whoopi Goldberg	Raven Symone
Zac, Taylor, and Isaac Hanson	Justin Timberlake
Jonas Brothers	Elijah Wood

OTHERS

Ansel Adams	Florence Nightingale
Susan B. Anthony	Thomas Paine
John James Audubon	Will Rogers
Clara Barton	Eleanor Roosevelt
Elizabeth Blackwell	Albert Schweitzer
Davy Crockett	Gloria Steinem
Mary Leakey	Serena and Venus Williams
Margaret Mead	Frank Lloyd Wright
John Muir	

FAMOUS HOMESCHOOLING PARENTS

Will Smith and Jada Pinkett Smith	Lisa Whelchel and Steve Cauble
John Travolta and Kelly Preston	

Further Resources on This Topic

Videos and links to homeschooled athletes
http://homeschooling.gomilpitas.com/weblinks/Famous.htm

18. Who should not homeschool?

I rarely tell a parent she shouldn't homeschool. I've heard lots of excuses from people why they do not homeschool, and I try to be supportive of whatever educational choices a parent makes because I expect the same in return from other people. There is something about the simple fact that we do homeschool, though, that makes some people feel inadequate, guilty, and defensive. . . . I can usually counter any argument against homeschooling with 40 reasons why a family should homeschool, even when the excuse seems so valid to the individual putting it forth. The short answer is that there should be no reason why a family shouldn't homeschool. The reality is that reasons exist, but each family has to base its own decision on whether those reasons are compelling enough.

—Carol Narigon, "Why I Shouldn't Homeschool,"
in *Home Education Magazine*

Are there people who should not homeschool? Yes, probably. However, it is rarely the ones who are actually doubting their ability. It is not the mother who says she would never have the patience, or is not organized enough, or intelligent enough—because all of that is easy to change or remedy. Single parenthood can be a complication but does not have to rule out homeschooling. Not having a college degree is far from a deciding factor as it is not required. Having an unsupportive spouse or partner can be a problem, but again, not an insurmountable one. Convincing a reluctant significant other takes work and dedication but is definitely possible. Angry divorce issues can make things uncomfortable and the issue of homeschooling can potentially cause custody complications down the road.

Perhaps the single most persuasive reason not to homeschool is if you do not really enjoy the company of your children. If this is sincerely true, than maybe home education is not your best choice. However, keep in mind the possibility that the reason you do not enjoy being with your kids may change if you get them out of the school environment. "Sometimes spending more time together helps a parent and child become close," writes Carol Narigon in *Home Education Magazine*. "After all, spending more time together is often the antidote for marital partners who have grown apart."

Further Resources on This Topic

Pros and cons of homeschooling
http://homeschooling.gomilpitas.com/weblinks/whynot.htm

What

Just for Laughs

You know you are a homeschool parent when...

you get to change more than diapers; you get to change their minds.

your child busts a lip, and after seeing she's okay, you round up some Scotch tape to capture some blood and look at it under the microscope.

your children never ever leave the *why?* stage.

you ask for a copier instead of a diamond tennis bracelet for your wedding anniversary.

you never have to drive your child's forgotten lunch to school.

the only debate about the school lunch program is whose turn it is to cook.

you cannot make it through a movie without pointing out the historical inaccuracies.

you (quickly) try to capture the huge bee that was knocked unconscious as it accidentally flew into your car window, so the kids can classify and inspect it.

you've got more books and bookcases than anyone you know.

the walls of your dining room are decorated with posters showing the U.S. presidents, the periodic table of elements, a map of the moon, a Spanish conjugation chart, and a copy of the Declaration of Independence.

your children are draped all over the furniture and they're reading... for the *fun* of it.

your children actually enjoy spending time with their family, even their siblings.

your children aren't embarrassed to be seen playing with someone younger than they are.

you've laughed out loud when someone asked you "What about socialization?"

19. What are the laws regarding homeschooling?

Get educated, stay informed, and get involved. Keep an eye on what your legislature is doing and take the time to go to testify on proposed bills that will affect you and your parental rights. Every state has a website about their legislature; take the time to find yours and check it over. You can track bills online and you also have the ability

to email your representatives and tell them what is on your mind. When election time rolls around find out what your candidates positions are on the issues that affect you. Vote!
— Judy Aron, Director of Research,
National Home Education Legal Defense

The most important thing to realize from the very beginning is that homeschooling is legal in every state of this nation. But each state has its own set of rules regarding homeschooling, so it is essential that you check out yours in order to have a clear understanding of them. How do you find out what your state's laws are? You can

- ask other homeschoolers
- contact your state homeschooling support group
- go online and do a search

Should you call your local public school system or Department of Education and ask them? It is not recommended. More often than not, they do not know the current laws. They also have a built-in bias that might spill over into their response.

Homeschooling laws differ from state to state in seven main areas:

- **Testing.** Do your children have to take standardized tests? If so, how often and at what grade levels? Who can administer them? How are scores reported?
- **Equivalency.** What is the minimum number of days you are required to teach? Typically it ranges from 132 to 188 (although new legislation may increase that number).
- **Records.** Do you have to keep attendance records? Any other types?
- **Registration.** Do you have to register with the state and/or your local school district? What happens if you do not comply?
- **Notification of intent to homeschool.** Is this required? If so, do you write a letter or fill out a form?

- **Curriculum.** Does your state require a name of the curriculum you are going to use for each subject? (Just because they ask does not mean you need to provide it.)
- **Parental competency level.** A few states may want to know if you have a GED, high school diploma, and/or college degree. Check with other homeschoolers in your region to make sure if there are any requirements in this area.

Once you know the laws, you will have a better idea of what you do and do not have to do. If you do not like your state's laws, you can work to change them by writing letters to your representatives, attending local and state committee meetings, and speaking out for change.

Further Resources on This Topic

"Homeschool Laws and Legalities," A to Z Home's Cool
http://homeschooling.gomilpitas.com/directory/Legalities.htm

"Homeschooling Laws," Successful Homeschooling
http://www.successful-homeschooling.com/homeschooling-laws
.html

20. What are the myths about homeschooling?

Many people are afraid of educational alternatives that they are not familiar with—it is easier to repeat misinformation or homeschool myths heard from others than it is to expend the energy to discover the facts for oneself.

—Homeschool Myths and Facts

Those who have been homeschooling for a while are constantly doing everything they can to fight the ongoing myths that surround home education. These myths lead to misunderstanding and confusion—and can make it harder for family and friends to support your homeschooling decision. Here are the top ten most common myths and why they are false.

Common Myth 1: Only hippies homeschool.
To say that only a particular group of people homeschools is inaccurate, because all types of people homeschool. People of different religions, ethnic groups, economic levels, educational backgrounds, and age homeschool.

Common Myth 2: Only religious people homeschool.
See above. This is one of the biggest myths surrounding homeschooling; as time passes, it becomes less and less accurate. People of all different religious beliefs—as well as those who are agnostic or atheist—choose to homeschool.

Common Myth 3: Homeschooling is schooling at home.
It can be, if that is the philosophy or method the family chooses, but it certainly is not required or inevitable. For a number of families, homeschooling has as little to do with the public school model as possible.

Common Myth 4: Homeschooling costs a lot of money.
This will be covered more in depth elsewhere, but the simple truth is that homeschooling does not need to cost a lot of money. How much you have to buy is up to you, and much of the material can be found at no to low cost.

Common Myth 5: Homeschooling is not legal.
We will examine this issue in detail later on, but yes, homeschooling is legal in all 50 states, all of which have their own rules to follow.

Common Myth 6: You need a teaching degree to homeschool.
Not true. In fact, some homeschooling parents who happen to have a teaching degree find that the degree gets in the way and makes homeschooling more difficult.

Common Myth 7: Homeschooled children will never learn to socialize.
Of all the myths surrounding the process of home education, this is the biggest one—and the most incorrect one. Children who are

homeschooled get out in the real world far more than kids stuck all day in a building with people the same age. Their socialization is different—and many homeschoolers believe it to be superior.

Common Myth 8: Homeschoolers never leave the house.

This is an offshoot of the previous myth—homeschoolers leave the house all the time. They go places with their families, they go to classes, to workshops, on field trips, to friends' houses, and much more. They play on teams, sing in choirs, participate in performances, and engage in every other activity young people enjoy.

Common Myth 9: Homeschoolers cannot go to college.

They can and they do. In fact, in recent years, admissions officers have begun actively to search out homeschoolers because these students typically do well in college. Homeschooled students may have to approach the admissions process a little differently, relying more on portfolios and essays than on test scores, but admission into college is virtually never a problem, even with the most prestigious universities.

Common Myth 10: Homeschoolers cannot get into the military.

Once again, yes they can and they do—in growing numbers.

There are other myths that surround homeschooling. When you make any assumption about the process, make sure that it is based on truth and personal observation—not just on what someone has said or read.

Further Resources on This Topic

"The Most Common Home-Schooling Myths Exposed and
     Explained," by Sarah Borroum
http://articles.familylobby.com/212-the-most-common
     -home-schooling-myths-exposed-.htm

"Homeschool Myths and Facts"
http://www.early-years-homeschool.com/homeschool-myths.html

21. What about socialization?

Home-schooled children are taking part in the daily routines of their communities. They are certainly not isolated; in fact, they associate with—and feel close to—all sorts of people. Home schooling parents can take much of the credit for this. For, with their children's long-term social development in mind, they actively encourage their children to take advantage of social opportunities outside the family. Home-schooled children are acquiring the rules of behavior and systems of beliefs and attitudes they need. They have good self-esteem and are likely to display fewer behavior problems than do other children. They may be more socially mature and have better leadership skills than other children as well. And they appear to be functioning effectively as members of adult society.

—Richard Medlin, Home Schooling and the
Question of Socialization[1]

Of all the questions in this book, this is the one that the curious or new homeschoolers ask most often. It is also the one that makes veteran homeschoolers grind their teeth and clench their jaws. Because of that, this answer is going to include a number of quotes from people to show their thoughts on the topic.

When people ask about socialization for homeschoolers, what they typically mean is one of two things. (1) How will they learn to interact with others? Or (2) How will they find friends? The answer to both questions is relatively simple.

How will my child learn to interact with others?

The interaction kids get in school is not realistic. Spending the entire day in one building with people the same age as you, who live in the same area as you, and who know the same people as you is not socializing. Socializing is meeting with, talking to, and interacting with people of all sorts—people of different backgrounds, ages,

---

[1]http://www.homeschool.com/articles/Keystone7/default.asp

races, personalities, opinions, appearance, and so on. By virtue of not having to be in school all day, homeschooled kids typically spend their hours out in the real world, interacting with all sorts of people. They socialize the way adults do and in the process they learn the skills that parents are hoping they will: how to be polite, respond to questions, carry on conversations, show respect, verbally articulate their thoughts, and all of the other skills socializing teaches. They learn it all realistically, not artificially.

How will my child find friends?

All young people, homeschooled or otherwise need friends. Peers are important; however, so is family. Homeschooling gives families a chance to increase and expand their bond such that siblings are often also (amazingly enough) friends. Homeschooling kids meet other kids through

- homeschooling support groups
- 4H clubs
- scouting or campfire groups
- other clubs and organizations
- YMCA and YWCA
- church or other religious venue
- volunteering
- community sports teams
- part time jobs
- community college classes
- other classes and workshops
- library
- homeschooling conferences
- other homeschooling friends' homes

The following are comments from a number of people about the issue of socialization and homeschooling. These comments make it clear that your child will have countless opportunities to learn social skills and to establish friendships—the true goals of socialization.

Homeschoolers, without the constraints of a six-hour school schedule, are extremely vulnerable to falling into the trap of too many outside activities and too much social interaction. This can be dangerous, especially if we hope to teach our children to appreciate and enjoy the quiet, reflective life.

—John Andersen, in *Asking Questions, Finding Answers*

Instead of being locked behind school gates in what some would consider an artificial setting characterized by bells, forced silence and age-segregation, homeschoolers frequently extend their everyday classroom to fire departments, hospitals, museums, repair shops, city halls, national parks, churches and colleges, where real community interaction and contacts are made. Dismantling the stereotype that home learners spend their days isolated from society at kitchen tables with workbooks in hand, NHERI reports that they actually participate in approximately five different social activities outside the home on a regular basis. Furthermore, researcher Dr. Linda Montgomery found that 78 percent of high school home learners were employed with paying jobs, while a majority engaged in volunteering and community service.

—Michael Haverluck, *Socialization: Homeschooling vs. Schools*[2]

[People] must believe that socializing is the most important job of public school. Since this is always the first question "inquiring minds" want to know, I can only assume this is important. No one asks me how I'm going to teach the kids to read, conjugate verbs, or dissect frogs, so presumably they trust in my ability to convey those important skills. I would like to point out, however, that what public school socializes your children to do is spend six hours sitting in a room with twenty-nine other people the same age during which they must pee and eat at the same time as well as line up to move from

---

[2]http://www.cbn.com/CBNnews/144135.aspx

room to room. If you know of any place but public school where this would be a useful skill, you let me know.

—Toast Floats blog[3]

Socialization is knowing how to act appropriately in various situations and is best taught by adults who care about the child. Socialization is not the same as having a social life. Remember this when you hear the dreaded "S" word from others. Your homeschooled kids will have as many friends and activities as they want and you allow (and likely more time than their PS peers to enjoy them). They will be socialized by their parents and other caring people who will help them learn appropriate behavior in different situations—at home, in public, in informal and formal activities. They will have many opportunities to learn and practice social skills as they will be interacting with the real world on a regular basis.

—"Socialization vs. Social Life"[4]

A family member asked my wife, "Aren't you concerned about his (our son's) socialization with other kids?" My wife gave this response: "Go to your local middle school, junior high, or high school, walk down the hallways, and tell me which behavior you see that you think our son should emulate." Good answer.

—Manfred Zysk, "Homeschooling and the Myth of Socialization"[5]

Research conducted by Michael Brady entitled Social Development in Traditionally Schooled and Homeschooled Children, a Case for Increased Parental Monitoring and Decreased Peer Interaction endorses this idea. Brady states, "There seems to be an overwhelming amount of evidence that children socialized in a peer-dominant environment are at higher risk for developing

---

[3]http://blog.toastfloats.com/2007/04/10-reasons-why-you-shouldnt-home school.html
[4]http://homeschooling.about.com/od/socialization/a/socialization.htm
[5]http://www.lewrockwell.com/orig/zysk1.html

social maladjustment issues than those that are socialized in a parent monitored environment."

In other words, socialization in homeschooling works better because children have more opportunities to be socialized through the modeling of good social behavior by caring adults rather than through peers, who do not know much more than they do. Parents give their kids the skills they need to interact with other people and also have the chance to protect their children.

—"What about Socialization?"[6]

By spending almost all of their school hours with children of the same age, kids find themselves becoming peer dependent (I need to ask Susan if this outfit looks good; Jayme told me to stop acting so stupid at lunch), competitive (I have to do better than them or I will not make the team), and pressured (Everyone else is trying pot and if I do not, they will think I am weird and will not like me anymore). They may find themselves labeled (geek, nerd, queer, lame, loser, suck up) and if they are unfortunate enough not to be among the elite group that is deemed popular, they may suffer from self-image and self-esteem problems. Is this the socialization you are afraid your children are missing out on? Is that what you want for your kids? Or, as John Holt writes in one of his books, "If there was no other reason for wanting to keep kids out of school, the social life would be reason enough."

—Tamra Orr, *Asking Questions, Finding Answers*

Further Resources on This Topic

"What about Socialization?"
http://www.homeschool.com/articles/Keystone7/default.asp

"Socialization: The 'S' Word," A to Z Home's Cool
http://homeschooling.gomilpitas.com/articles/042998.htm

---

[6]http://www.homeschool.com/articles/Socialization/default.asp

22. What qualifications do my spouse/partner or I need in order to homeschool?

Education would be so much more effective if its purpose was to ensure that by the time they leave school, every boy and girl should know how much they do not know and be imbued with a lifelong desire to know it.

—William Haley, newspaper reporter

The qualifications you need to homeschool may not be the ones you had imagined. For example, you do not need to have a teaching degree or any other kind of college degree. The qualifications that you do need, however, include

- patience
- time
- flexibility
- an open mind
- a good sense of humor
- the ability to share material
- the ability to learn material
- the ability to listen to your children
- the ability to enjoy being with your children
- a desire to be with your children
- the ability to get along with your children
- the ability to keep papers in order
- the willingness to search our curricula and other material

Almost every parent has every one of these abilities, although most likely in varying amounts. Which are your strongest traits? Which do you think could use some work? How about your partner? Often your weaknesses are his or her strengths and vice versa. Depending on each other to help fill in those shakier parts is part of a good relationship—and of homeschooling.

Further Resources on This Topic

"The Myth of Teacher Qualifications," by Chris Klicka, Homeschool
   Legal Defense Association
http://www.hslda.org/docs/nche/000002/00000214.asp

"The Main Qualification for Home Schooling Is a Desire to Teach
   Your Children at Home," by Paulla Estes
http://www.happynews.com/living/schoolchoices/start-home
   -schooling.htm

23. What are learning styles?

*Most parents assume their children learn exactly like they do. For
instance, if the parents are visual learners, it's not at all uncommon
for them to expect their kids to be visual learners, too. But children
often have different learning styles than their parents. Furthermore,
they often have different learning styles than their siblings. The
sooner you understand learning styles and which learning styles
your children have, the sooner you'll be able to connect with them on
a deeper and more meaningful level, and the sooner you'll be able to
teach them effectively.*

—"Why Are Learning Styles Important?"[7]

When you were in school, how did you learn new material the best?
Was it from listening to the teacher explain a concept (auditory)? Was
it from reading the information in a textbook (visual)? Perhaps it was
from doing an experiment in a lab (kinesthetic). The answer to this will
give you a clue as to what kind of learner you are. Understanding what
kind of learner you are will also help you to understand what kind of
learners your children might be.

---

[7]http://www.sonlight.com/learning-styles.html

Learning styles, also called multiple intelligences, are typically divided into seven different categories, according to Dr. Howard Gardner, Harvard psychologist and author of *Frames of Mind*. Look over the following chart:

LEARNING STYLE	POSSIBLE CAREERS	PREFERRED ACTIVITIES	LEARNING TOOLS
linguistic	author	reading, playing word games, making up or writing stories and poems	computers, books, CDs, lectures
logical/ mathematical	accountant	abstract reasoning, puzzle solving	logic games, mysteries
spatial/visual	architect	drawing, reading maps	charts and graphics, photographs, drawings, multimedia
musical	musician	singing, speaking rhythmically	musical instruments, music, radio, CDs
bodily/kinesthetic	dancer	moving, making things, role playing, hands-on learning	arts and crafts material
interpersonal	teacher, salesperson	talking to others, working as part of a team	group activities
intrapersonal	writer	introspective	independent study

Do you see your children in these descriptions? Naturally, they will blend the different styles but most people tend to have one or two primary styles. Why is it important for you to know your children's learning styles? Because it will help you choose appropriate curricula. For example, if your child tends to be linguistic, workbooks can be very effective but puzzles or mazes may not. It will also help you design activities for your children because an interpersonal child will be much more interested than an intrapersonal child in going on field trips or joining a homeschooling sports team.

It may be that you have no idea what learning style fits your children because you have not had the chance to observe them closely enough. Just make it part of that trial-and-error process you're going through. Watch what works best for your children and what does not, what they respond to and what not, what they understand immediately and what not. At the same time, take note and learn more about your own learning style. As you work with your children, knowing what works most effectively for you will also be helpful.

Further Resources on This Topic

"Learning Styles Quiz," from Rebecca Kochenderfer's *Homeschooling and Loving It*
http://www.homeschool.com/articles/Ablaze5/default.asp

Learning styles
http://homeschooling.gomilpitas.com/weblinks/assets.htm

Multiple intelligences
http://www.tecweb.org/styles/gardner.html

24. What is unschooling?

I am beginning to suspect all elaborate and special systems of education. They seem to me to be built upon the supposition that every child is a kind of idiot who must be taught to think. Whereas, if the child is left to himself, he will think more and better, if less showily. Let him go and come freely, let him touch real things and combine his impressions for himself, instead of sitting indoors at a little round table, while a sweet-voiced teacher suggests that he build a stone wall with his wooden blocks, or make a rainbow out of strips of colored paper, or plant straw trees in bead flower-pots. Such teaching fills the mind with artificial associations that must be got rid of, before the child can develop independent ideas out of actual experience.

—Anne Sullivan, Helen Keller's teacher[8]

As mentioned earlier in this book, unschooling is one of many different methods of homeschooling. It is on the far end of the spectrum, being more relaxed or unstructured than the rest. It is difficult to explain what it is because every family approaches and employs it differently. It is more a philosophy than a way of teaching. Perhaps writer and homeschooler Sandra Dodd puts it best when she says, "Stop thinking schoolishly. Stop acting teacherishly. Stop talking about learning as though it's separate from life."

In *What I Do Monday*, John Holt wrote, "We can see that there is no difference between living and learning, that living is learning, that it is impossible, and misleading, and harmful to think of them as being separate. We say to children, 'you come to school to learn.' We say to each other [educators], 'our job is to teach children to learn.' But the children have been learning all the time, for all of their lives before they met us. What is more, they are very likely to be much better at learning than most of us who plan to teach them something."

In *The Unschooling Handbook*, Mary Griffith attempts to pinpoint how unschoolers live. She writes, "To unschoolers, learning is as natural as breathing—as worthwhile for its own sake, something that happens all the time, rather than in a specific place at a specific time, according to a set schedule. Curiosity is a constant, not to be denied because the setting is not overly educational or the topic does not fall into a familiar school category. Unschoolers realize that different people learn different subjects at different times," she continues, "they tend not to judge individuals based on how 'smart' they are or what grade they're in."

Unschoolers believe that education is child-led—that by trusting children to learn, explore, and discover, they will be educated. When a

---

[8]http://www.unschooling.com/

child becomes interested in a topic, parents act as guides, helping their kids find the right materials to support that fascination. Instead of studying math, science, history, and English, children study turtles and in the process, learn about the biology of the creature, write a report, study the countries where they live, draw pictures of different species—covering all the academic bases by pursuing the child's original interests.

Unschooling does not mean never using textbooks or flash cards—it means using them if that is what your child likes to use to learn. (And yes, there are kids who really like them—and ask for them—when they are given the choice rather than being coerced into using them.) It means following their lead. How do you know if they are learning? As they say at Unschooling.com,

> *"You will know by listening to them speak, by watching them play, just by being with them. You will know they are leaning at 8 the same way you knew they were learning at 18 months. You will see them use their skills and knowledge. This does take some effort on the part of the parent. The information is not contained on a worksheet or within a report. It is not all nice and neat and tied up with a grade. It's spread out over the course of the day while the children are living their lives. You have to be observant and tuned into your child, in order to know. The nice thing about this is that it's great fun to observe your children so closely, to be so in tune with their lives. It brings contentment to both parent and child to know each other so well."*

Unschooling requires a great deal of trust on the part of parents, and few novice homeschoolers are able to adopt this radical way of educating. However, a growing number of homeschoolers end up here and their only wish is that they had started following this philosophy much sooner.

Further Resources on This Topic

www.unschooling.com

Unschooling information and a link to live text chats with unschoolers
http://sandradodd.com/unschooling

25. What records do I need to keep?

Your records can be as simple as a daily journal or as elaborate as a purchased computer program or notebook system. If you are part of a support group or ISP, you probably will have set requirements and forms provided, but you will need to decide on how to keep track of your daily work to make reporting easier and more efficient.
—Beverly Hernandez, "Homeschool Record Keeping"[9]

What records you need to maintain depends somewhat on what your state requires. A number of states ask you to keep attendance records (not that they are ever likely to see them) so that you can document the equivalency requirement (educating so many hours per day/days per year). Some expect you to keep material for use in transcripts and others want you to have portfolios that summarize work done each year.

How you keep your records is primarily up to you. The state almost never asks to see anything. One of the best, easiest, and least expensive ways to keep records is to buy a teacher's record book at any teacher's supply store and record information in it. You can jot down what subjects you covered with each child. A simple set of folders and notebooks can also be used to save worksheets, drawings, and other paperwork.

You can create your own record-keeping system or purchase one. How much you include in it depends greatly on your state rules, as well as on your own personal preferences. Some parents are very detailed; some just jot down brief notes. Still others, who live in states that do not require any records, simply do not keep any at all.

If you decide to put together your own system, here are some basic suggestions.

- **Keep a journal.** You can keep a daily journal that reports what you taught and what your kids have done.
- **Put together a portfolio.** A portfolio is a multimedia collection of what each child has accomplished and can include

---

[9]http://homeschooling.about.com/cs/recordkeeping/a/backrecord.htm

everything from projects, rewards, drawings, and research papers to test results, artwork, and certificates.

- **Create a transcript.** A transcript is a simple listing of the classes taken or the material covered and the grade and credit hours given. Such a record will be useful if your child reenters public school or needs a transcript for college admission.

If you are not sure how to keep records, what your state requires, or what you are comfortable doing, try talking to people in your support group and see what they do. Remember that this is trial and error here too, and be ready to buy a couple of record-keeping systems that you end up throwing out or giving away because they just do not suit you and your family.

Further Resources on This Topic

Excel spreadsheet for homeschooling
http://homeschooling.gomilpitas.com/articles/092698.htm

Other templates for homeschool planners
http://homeschooling.gomilpitas.com/materials/SW4Records.htm

26. What if my spouse/partner does not support homeschooling?

Often the objection I hear from discerning mothers is, "I would love to home school, but my husband will not let me. He thinks the children will be weird." My advice to the mother is to drag dad to the nearest mall and find the weirdest young person there. You know, the kid with nuts and bolts drilled into his face, tattoos all over his body, and purple hair. Go right up and ask him if he is home schooled! Let's face it; any honest father will have to admit that all the really weird kids attend institutional schools.

—"No Fighting, No Biting"[10]

---

[10]http://nofightingnobiting.blogspot.com/2007/08/husband-nervous-about-homeschooling.html

Homeschooling really is a joint effort: Like anything else in parenting, it works best when it is a unified decision. If one partner is against the idea, that can make everything more difficult. Typically, it is the mother who wants to homeschool and the father who is not so sold on the idea. Occasionally, it is the other way around.

The key to solving the problem is to find out exactly what the partner's objection is and then to do whatever you can to respond to that issue. For example, if it is the mother who is objecting, it tends to be because she is worried that she will not be able to cope with the added responsibility homeschooling will bring into her life. If it is the father, it may be because he is worried that, by homeschooling, his children will not have a solid enough education to compete in today's world. Maybe he is concerned about the cost of it or that his kids will be looked at as strange.

Figuring out the issue that is most worrisome is the first step. The second is to sit down and discuss it. How have you worked out problems or disagreements before? Whatever worked for you in the past will most likely work for you now. Arrange to go out to dinner and talk or stay up late and discuss it—do whatever it takes to find a way to come to an agreement.

The fact that both of you have the same goal in mind—the well-being of your children—will help give you a foundation to work from. From there, you can talk as well as share reading material, talk with other homeschoolers, or even attend a conference together. Consider a compromise: Agree to try homeschooling for a limited amount of time (at least a few months) and see how it works out. A solution can almost always be found if everyone stays open-minded, logical, and friendly.

Further Resources on This Topic

"Help! How Can I Convince my Husband to Let Me Homeschool the Kids?" by Denise Wilms

http://ezinearticles.com/?Help!-How-Can-I-Convince-My-Husband -to-Let-Me-Home-School-the-Kids?&id=1310956

27. What if my child does not want to be homeschooled?

My daughter was in tears this morning, telling me she didn't want to
be homeschooled anymore. I couldn't believe it! I immediately started
panicking at how I was going to enroll in school in the middle of the
year. However, I stopped and asked her simply, "Why?" She replied,
"I want to ride the school bus!" That was it—just the bus. The next
week, we took a ride on a city bus and she was thrilled. That was the
last we heard about going to school.

—Lea, homeschooling mom

Homeschooling is not only a parental decision but one that involves your children's thoughts and emotions. How they feel about going to school at home is important, especially if they have been in school before or are old enough to have a strong opinion on the matter.

If your child is not one of those who is thrilled to have the chance to stop going to public school, it is important not to ignore her feelings—or completely give in to them. Instead, just as with a partner who is less than thrilled with the idea, try to find out the primary reason behind the unhappiness. Sometimes it really is as simple as a child wanting to ride the bus, get new school clothes, or buy new pens, folders, and other supplies. Other times the reason is more serious, such as a concern that he will not be able to spend time with his friends, be on the football team, or get the transcripts he needs in order to go to the college of his choice.

Whatever the reason, even if it seems somewhat trivial to you, you can rest assured it is most likely not trivial to your children. Approach their concerns with respect and listen to their reasoning. Then, address it as best you can. If he is upset because he cannot be on the tennis team, research together and find a community team he can join. If she is concerned that she will not be able to hang out with her friends, immediately make plans for those friends to come for a sleepover, to watch a movie, or to go to a favorite place to eat. There are virtually no issues that cannot be solved if you work on it together.

Next, involve your children in the homeschooling plan you are making. Talk about what they want to learn and encourage them to make a list of topics they would like to explore, books they'd like to read, places they would like to go, games they would like to play, and other activities. Often this is exciting for them as they begin to realize how much freedom they have to choose their own curriculum.

Take time also to remind your children of what they can avoid while homeschooling—cafeteria food, pop quizzes, public showers, long bus rides—whatever it was that they particularly did not enjoy. Sometimes just the realization that they do not have to rush out of the house every morning or sit inside on a gorgeous spring day is enough to sell them on the idea of homeschooling.

Further Resources on This Topic

Not Back to School Camp for teen homeschoolers
www.nbtsc.org

Teen homeschool hangout
www.teenhomeschoolhang.com/phpBB3/

28. What if my child is already enrolled in public school?

Dear Mr. Principal, I am keeping Timothy Michaels at home to homeschool. Thanks!

—Mrs. Michaels

If your children are already in school and you make the decision to homeschool, you will need to send their school a Letter of Intent to Homeschool. It is a simple letter to write and does not require any special form. You simply address it to the principal, providing your children's full names and stating that your children will no longer be attending because you are planning to homeschool.

Although not all states require this letter, it is considered a good idea to send it because otherwise the school may consider your children truant and come knocking on your door. Keep a copy of your letter, in case the school claims not to have received it or better yet, send it certified/return receipt to prove the school received it.

Further Resources on This Topic

Sample Letter of Intent
http://www.cthomeschoolnetwork.org/CtLaw-Letter%20of%20
    Withdrawal.htm

"Withdrawing your Child from Public or Private School Mid-Year"
http://www.hsc.org/midyear.html

29. What if my child is doing well in school?

Do not be misled into believing that getting good grades is the same thing as doing well in school. There are so many advantages to homeschooling that go far beyond G.P.A. Allow all of your children the chance to reap the benefits of a home education.

—Lea, homeschooling mom

It may seem logical that if your child is in public school and doing well, you should let things be. There is merit to that idea—but too many times a child is not doing well in all facets of school and could easily benefit from being homeschooled. Perhaps she is making great grades but is having trouble making friends. Perhaps he is popular but is bored in class. Maybe she is on the sports team but keeps having discipline issues.

Succeeding in school does not necessarily mean enjoying school. Even if your children are doing well in school, they might do even better in homeschool. Talk to your children about the idea of homeschooling. You may be surprised at how pleased they are at the chance to try something different.

Further Resources on This Topic

"The Benefits (and Disadvantages) of Homeschooling"
http://www.sonlight.com/before-you-start-homeschooling.html

"Benefits to Homeschooling: A Growing List from Our Homeschool
    Family to Yours"
http://www.homeschool-curriculum-savings.com/benefits-to-home
    schooling.html

"Benefits of Homeschooling"
http://home-school.lovetoknow.com/Benefits_of_Homeschooling

30. What does the term deschooling or decompressing mean?

Deschooling is not just the child recovering from school damage. It's also the parents exploring their own school and childhood damage and proactively changing their thinking until the paradigm shift happens.

—Robyn Coburn[11]

In an article she wrote about deschooling, Sandra Dodd wrote, "Once upon a time a confident and experienced scholar went to the best Zen teacher he knew, to apply to be his student. The master offered tea, and he held out his cup. While the student recited his knowledge and cataloged his accomplishments to date, the master poured slowly. The bragging continued, and the pouring continued, until the student was getting a lapful of tea, and said, "My cup is full!" The master smiled and said, "Yes, it is. And until you empty yourself of what you think you know, you will not be able to learn."[11]

This story illustrates some of the thought behind *deschooling*. This term is used to refer to that period of time your child has to go through after being in public school and then coming home to homeschool. It is quite a bit like the decompression that deep-sea divers have to go through before rising to the surface. Do it too fast and you will pay a painful price. Kids who have been in public school may have trouble handling homeschooling in the beginning, especially if you follow the relaxed or unschooling methods. Most kids have been told what to study, when to study, how to study, where to study, and why to study every day of their lives since they turned six. Suddenly having the freedom to choose what to read, do, think, and learn can be very exciting—

---

[11]http://sandradodd.com/deschooling

but also a little intimidating. Think of a pet that has been kept inside the same room of the house all of its life. When it is finally let out, it may be thrilled but also rather scared. The same could be true here. On the other hand, your child may rejoice and want to run through the house screaming, "I'm free, I'm free at last!"

If you are bringing your child home to homeschool—especially if you are doing so because the child has been struggling academically—please allowing some time to relax and deschool a bit before launching into a curriculum. As one site states,

> *Rather than rushing out to buy text-books or worrying about follow-ing a curriculum when beginning home educating, many families find that it's best to begin with a period of de-schooling. If your child has had problems in school such as bullying, or exam stress, it's par-ticularly important to take time to relax together as a family, to read, to discuss issues, to talk about goals and ambitions, and to think about what education means to you.*
>
> —H. Ed. info, "Deschooling to Start Home Education"

How much time do your children need to deschool? It depends on them, their age, personality, how much they struggled in school, and how long they attended. As the Home-Ed.info site states,

> *It has been informally established that, the longer a child has been in school, the more time he or she needs to unwind and "de-school" before beginning any formal study. A month per year of formal schooling is sometimes given—so a child of ten who has been in school for five years may need up to five months of relaxing at home without any guided study. Of course this varies from child to child, but it is vital not to rush straight into a program of education, par-ticularly if your child has left school after a lot of stress. Building family relationships and self-esteem is far more important.*[12]

---

[12]http://home-ed.info/home_ed_articles/deschooling.htm

Bring them home, sit back, relax, and enjoy their company. Forget homework and classes for a while and let them remember what it's like to enjoy learning instead of being forced to do so.

Further Resources on This Topic

Deschooling
http://homeschooling.gomilpitas.com/weblinks/deschooling.htm

"Deschooling for Parents," by Sandra Dodd
http://sandradodd.com/deschooling

31. What role does the Internet play in homeschooling?

It all comes down to trust. Trusting your children. Since they were born we have raised them with respect, trusted their good sense, and basically tried to treat them as individuals with worthwhile opinions and feelings to be respected. When some action of theirs comes up that we are uncomfortable with, we discuss it with them, give reasons for our unease, and listen to their responses. It is a give and take, with listening occurring on both sides. It's not always easy, and I know we have not always been successful. But we trust them, and I hope they trust us. They have not shown us any reason to distrust them; therefore we continue to do so. And this trust includes computers and Internet usage.

> —Karen Gibson, "Leaping from the Box"

The role of computers in homeschooling mirrors the role of computers in almost everything else in today's electronic society: with each passing year, it becomes more important. Can you successfully homeschool without a computer at home? Yes. Do you want to? Not likely.

Having a computer in the house that your homeschooling child can easily and readily access is not a requirement but it is a strong recommendation. Computers fill so many different roles today and this is certainly true in the home education realm. Here are some of the primary ways a home computer will be put to use:

- **Basic computer skills.** Knowing how to use a computer, including surfing the Internet, is considered a basic skill today. Regardless of what field your children might pursue, they will need to know their way around a computer. They will need to have keyboarding skills, as well as familiarity with various computer programs.
- **Social networking.** In today's world, a great deal of peer communication goes on via the Internet. Whether it is through email, websites, chat rooms, or networks such as Facebook® or MySpace®, young people keep in touch with each other online. While precautions have to be taken and all kids should be taught the rules of Internet safety, this venue of socialization is an important one that computers can provide.
- **Correspondence courses/distance learning.** The courses available online keep growing so fast that it is almost impossible to make a statement about them and get it published before it is obsolete. For example, in the 2006–2007 academic year, 97% of public two-year institutions and 89% of public four-year institutions throughout the nation offered college-level distance education courses.[13] By the year 2013, experts believe more than 18 million students will be enrolled in distance education courses.
- **Local community college classes.** Many homeschoolers choose to enroll in local classes and a good portion of the choices are offered only online.
- **Internet-based homeschooling programs.** A growing number of companies are creating online programs specifically for homeschoolers. Their lessons, as well as teacher support, are available online.

---

[13]http://nces.ed.gov/fastfacts/display.asp?id=80

- **Research.** Learning how to do quality research online is an indispensable skill to develop, and the computer can help with this. Your kids can use the computer to research everything from undersea life or favorite authors to European recipes to French slang. They can also use the Internet for researching colleges, going on virtual field trips, and more.

- **Composition and writing skills.** Writing assignments of any kind, whether a book report, a research paper, an essay or journal entry, can be done on a computer. For young children who are inspired to write but struggle with penmanship, the computer is especially helpful. Knowing how to use Microsoft Office® or other writing programs is an essential skill when it comes to job searching, college applications, and more.

- **Creating unit studies.** If you are going to create unit studies for your kids, the Internet will be invaluable in looking up resources, ordering library materials, downloading free worksheets and activities, finding crafts and other activities, and more.

Do not let the lack of a home computer be the sole reason you choose not to homeschool. There are always alternatives: you can teach your child quite well without one, perhaps supplementing it with computers at the local college, library, or any of the dozens of coffee shops with Wi-Fi. You might also give some thought to setting aside funds until you can add a computer to your house. In the meantime, old-fashioned textbooks work just wonderfully!

Further Resources on This Topic

"The Advantages of Using a Computer in Homeschooling," by
Brenda Hoffman
http://hubpages.com/hub/theadvantagesofusingacomputerinhome
schooling

"Computers and the Internet for Your Homeschool (Unschool)
Curriculum," by Karen Gibson
http://www.leapingfromthebox.com/art/kmg/computers.html

32. What is a typical homeschooling day like?

"When it comes to a typical day in homeschooling, there simply is no such thing!"

—Lea, homeschooling mom

Now that you have read about a third of this book, you already know that there is no such thing as a typical homeschooling day, because every single family does things differently. A structured homeschooler is definitely going to have a different day than those who unschool, for example. The beauty of homeschooling is that you can tailor it to whatever fits your life. If you work over the weekend but have part of the week off, you can homeschool then. If you work the late shift, you can adjust the times you homeschool. Everything is yours to customize as you see fit.

While no two days are going to be just alike, there will be a couple of common threads. For example, most homeschooling families will

- spend a good portion of the day together in educational and noneducational activities, and
- have some kind of activity planned, from running errands to attending classes to visiting friends to volunteering.

One of the best ways to explore a typical homeschool day is to go online and simply put those words into the search box. Dozens of examples, many of them personal blogs, will pop up. As you click on them and read through, you will most likely be struck by the fact that no two are exactly alike. Therein lies one of the biggest advantages of home education—you can make it whatever you want it to be.

Further Resources on This Topic

Creating your own homeschooling schedule
http://www.homeschooling-ideas.com/daily-homeschool-schedule
.html

33. What are the disadvantages of homeschooling?

When you approach the issue of home schooling you must examine both sides. Sure, there are plenty of advantages, but if you forget to look into the disadvantages, you may be setting yourself up for failure.

—"Disadvantages of Home Schooling"[14]

Of course there are downsides to homeschooling—depending on how you look at them. For example, the first one cited on many websites is that you will have to commit a great deal of your time to your children. In many ways, this is true but is that necessarily a bad thing? Would you rather be spending it with coworkers or strangers? Some parents may not enjoy their children's company; this can be a serious disadvantage. As you will discover, however, there are ways to make spending time with your kids more enjoyable for the whole family when you homeschool.

You will have to learn a lot and study in order to help your children learn material—is that bad? Learning more about your world is usually perceived as a good thing.

You may not be able to work a full-time job outside of the house while homeschooling, especially if your children are young. This can be hard on the family income and entail some sacrifices but again, that is not all bad. Imagine not having to leave the house every day, all dressed up!

Homeschooling will cost money, but it does not have to cost the fortune that some websites seem to imply. As you will see later in this

---

[14]http://www.articlesbase.com/homeschooling-articles/disadvantages-of-home-schooling-59112.html

book (Section 6, Question 71), the cost of materials is extremely variable and manageable.

You may have to be a little extra creative when it comes to creating transcripts, filling out college admission forms, and finding a driver education program, but none of these issues is difficult—they just take some time and effort.

The benefits of homeschooling are many and the downsides are few. Go online and read some of the perspectives of others and see what you think. The informed decision is always the wisest one.

Further Resources on This Topic

"Here are 10 Disadvantages of Homeschooling"
http://www.successful-homeschooling.com/disadvantages-of-home
schooling.html

"Homeschooling Pros and Cons"
http://homeschooling.suite101.com/article.cfm/homeschooling_
pros_and_cons

34. What are the most important supplies I need for homeschooling?

What children need is not new and better curricula but access to more and more of the real world; plenty of time and space to think over their experiences, and to use fantasy and play to make meaning out of them; and advice, road maps, guidebooks, to make it easier for them to get where they want to go (not where we think they ought to go) and to find out what they want to find out.

—John Holt, Teach Your Own

The supplies you need for homeschooling effectively and thoroughly depend on several factors:

- how many children you have
- how old they are

- what your budget is
- how much access you have to libraries, museums, zoos, and other resources
- what homeschooling method you are using (the more structured, the more supplies you will likely need)

Keeping those factors in mind, here are the things you will most likely need to have on hand:

- public library cards
- memberships to area museums, zoos, and so on
- subscriptions to homeschooling magazines
- subscriptions to educational magazines
- membership in local and state homeschooling organizations
- a home computer
- board games
- decks of cards
- crayons, pens, and pencils
- paper of all colors, shapes, and sizes
- arts and crafts supplies
- puzzles
- a globe or atlas and maps
- mass transit passes
- books, books, and more books

What about textbooks? school desks? workbooks? red grading pencils? a teacher's record books? All of these can be helpful and you might want to use them, but they are not required.

Where can you find these materials? You can get them locally or online—or a mixture of both. Possible sources are:

- garage sales
- thrift stores
- teacher's supply stores
- bookstores

- libraries
- catalogs
- homeschooling magazines
- other homeschoolers
- curriculum fairs and swaps

Once you have everything on these lists, you can begin homeschooling children of any age. As you experiment with different curricula and learn your children's learning style, preferences, and personal interests, you will develop a better idea of what you need to add to your supply cabinet. In the meantime, this will get you started.

Further Resources on This Topic

Homeschooling supplies
www.timberdoodle.com

Homeschooling materials and equipment
www.homeschoolingsupply.com

35. *What do students really* need *to know?*

It is as true now as it was then that no matter what tests show, very little of what is taught in school is learned, very little of what is learned is remembered, and very little of what is remembered is used. The things we learn, remember, and use are the things we seek out or meet in the daily, serious, nonschool parts of our lives.
—John Holt, *How Children Fail*

This is a huge question and very few of the answers can be found in the typical public school classroom. Robert Heinlein once wrote, "A human being should be able to change a diaper, plan an invasion, butcher a hog, conn a ship, design a building, write a sonnet, balance accounts, build a wall, set a bone, comfort the dying, take orders, give orders, cooperate, act alone, solve equations, analyze a new problem, pitch manure, program a computer, cook a tasty meal, fight efficiently, die gallantly. Specialization is for insects." Perhaps he was right.

What children really need to know depends a great deal on their age and on their circumstances:

- Children need to know basic survival skills.
- Children need to know they are loved.
- Children need to know they are safe.
- Children need to know how to communicate clearly.
- Children need to know how to find information.
- Children need to know they are capable of learning what is required for living in today's world.

Arguments can be made that children need to know how to read, do basic math, and have a grasp of history and other academics—and there is truth to that. But the best way to introduce all of these subjects is through real-life experience that shows the validity of the material, rather than through abstract lessons acquired while sitting at a desk.

As you consider what your children need to know, do your best to get away from the public school model of what is needed. Instead, think about what you want your children to be able to do on a daily basis. What skills and concepts do they need? Start there. Do not worry if what you are teaching is a grade above or below their actual age. Base it on their interest and ability instead. After all, when you are taught a new skill as an adult that is how you do it. No one tells you that you cannot learn a fascinating new idea because you are too old or too young. It should be the same for your children.

Further Resources on This Topic

"The Ten Most Important Things You Need to Know about Homeschooling"
http://www.homeschool.com/articles/mostimportant/default.asp

36. *What if my child and I argue?*

Accept that conflicts are normal and natural. You cannot always avoid conflicts, but you can always decide to manage conflicts with a positive attitude.

—Barbara Gibson, "Parent-Teen Conflicts"[15]

Homeschooling can do many amazing things for you and your family, but it is not a miracle cure and it definitely cannot guarantee that you will not argue with your kids anymore. Unfortunately there is no such guarantee—unless, perhaps, you live in separate households, and with cellphones, instant messaging, and texting, even that is doubtful.

You will still have disagreements with your kids—especially if you have emotional teenagers who sometimes get upset with you just for saying *Good morning* in the wrong tone of voice. But you may just find that your relationship does smooth out and improve through homeschooling. Children who have been in school for years and may have been unhappy there, perhaps dealing with peer pressure, bullying, or other stressors, may have been so miserable that it spilled over into the household and your relationship. You might have spent time arguing about going to school, completing homework, and other academic issues as well. If any of these have been the case, you may very well find that the number of arguments in your house decreases once you begin homeschooling.

Perhaps you are worried that the source of your arguments will be homeschooling itself. That is understandable. If you do indeed find that homeschooling triggers a disagreement between you and your child, it is time *not* to give up on the idea of homeschooling but to ask yourself what can be changed to make things less tense. Often changing the hours, subject, or most often style of your homeschooling can improve things. If you are working with a teen, try asking what he or she wants out of education. Listen to the input and

---

[15]http://parentingmethods.suite101.com/article.cfm/calm_parentteen_conflicts

respect it. If children see that you are taking the information seriously, they are more likely to feel they have some control and influence and will be less frustrated.

Further Resources on This Topic

"Avoiding Arguments and Power Struggles with your Kids"
http://life.familyeducation.com/behavioral-problems/punishment/
    42960.html

"How to Never Argue with your Child Again"
http://www.kidsraisedright.com/effective-parenting/effective-parenting
    -tips/how-to-never-argue-with-your-child-again/

37. What if my child refuses to read or write?

About reading, children learn something much more difficult than reading without instruction—namely, to speak and understand their native language. I do not think they they would or could learn it if they were instructed. I think reading instruction is the enemy of reading.
                                        —John Holt, *A Life Worth Living:*
                                            Selected Letters of John Holt

Reading and writing are two core skills that your children will need to learn. Too often, however, parents are so concerned about their kids learning them that they force them to do so before they truly are ready. This can result in difficulties and learning problems along the way or, if nothing else, lead your children to believe that reading and writing are boring and unpleasant chores.

Let us look at each of these skills for a moment. Reading is typically taught at age six, but some children learn how to do so earlier—and some later, if allowed. The average child may learn to walk at the age of one, but your child is not gifted if he does it at 10 months or handicapped if he does it at 14 months. It just means that that was when the child was ready. Similarly, children are ready to read at different ages, and forcing them to begin too early can be damaging. Waldorf schools, for example, teach reading years later than do traditional public schools. Why? "There is evidence that normal, healthy children who learn to read relatively late are not disadvantaged by this, but rather are able quickly to catch up with, and may overtake, children who have learned to read early," writes Colin Price in *Five Frequently Asked Questions*.[16] "Additionally, they are much less likely to develop the 'tiredness toward reading' that many children taught to read at a very early age experience later on. Instead there is lively interest in reading and learning that continues into adulthood. If reading is not pushed, a healthy child will pick it up quite quickly and easily," he continues. "Some Waldorf parents become anxious if their child is slow to learn to read. Eventually these same parents are overjoyed at seeing their child pick up a book and not put it down and become from that moment a voracious reader. Each child has his or her own optimal time for 'taking off.' Feelings of anxiety and inferiority may develop in a child who is not reading as well as her peers. Often this anxiety is picked up from parents concerned about the child's progress. It is important that parents should deal with their own and their child's apprehensions."

A number of homeschooling parents have reported that their children learned to read as early as four and as late as thirteen. "I have four children," says one homechooling mother. "Two taught themselves how to read at six. The other two learned—finally—at thirteen. All four of them read at the same level and above grade level today."

Children raised in a household where there are many books on the shelves, and parents who read out loud and read for pleasure themselves, are going to read. They simply may do it later and differently than parents are used to. Be patient and lead by example. It is pushing that turns kids off. Be sure to allow them the chance to pick their own

---

[16]http://www.whywaldorfworks.org/02_W_Education/faq_about.asp

reading material too—do not force classics on reluctant readers. Let them read magazines, game manuals, graphic novels, manga, whatever works. In time, they will make more literary choices or at least be able to understand the titles you assign them.

What about writing? Penmanship is a tough lesson to teach today, especially to young boys, who would rather have a tooth pulled than pick up a pencil and write. In today's electronic age, keyboarding is becoming the norm and handwriting is becoming a lost art. Being able to write legibly is still important, however, so basic penmanship is a good skill. Forcing kids to write every day, however, can have negative results. For example, kids who might want to create stories, poems, and other projects might not even try if they have to do write it by hand instead of on a computer.

Finding ways to make writing fun is often another important key. Having to keep a journal or diary may thrill some kids and terrify others. Other ideas include writing letters to friends and family far away, joining National Novel Writing Month in November (http://www.nanowrimo.org/), and writing and illustrating a comic book. Of course, your taking a red pencil and marking all the mistakes may be enough to kill a child's interest in writing. Instead, encourage them to do whatever kind of writing they want and instead of grading it, read and discuss it. As they mature, your children's spelling and grammar will improve, especially with helpful guidance rather than failing grades.

Further Resources on This Topic

"Helping your Homeschooler Learn to Read," by Isabel Shaw
http://school.familyeducation.com/home-schooling/reading/
    38692.html

"Homeschooling Reluctant Writers and Children Who Hate to Write,"
    by Julie Shepherd Knapp
http://www.homeschooldiner.com/subjects/language_arts/writing/
    reluctant/main.html

38. *What is the Charlotte Mason method?*

A child is a person in whom all possibilities are present—present now at this very moment—not to be educed after many years and efforts manifold on the part of the educator.

—Charlotte Mason[17]

Charlotte Mason (1842–1923) was a British educator who developed her own philosophy of education based on three principles which she characterized as "an atmosphere, a discipline, and a life."

Atmosphere refers to the surroundings in which a child grows up. ("The child breathes the atmosphere emanating from his parents; that of the ideas which rule their own lives.") *Discipline* refers to the development of good habits, especially those of character. Mason likens habits to a set of train tracks laid down by the parents for the child to follow into adulthood. ("It rests with [the parent] to consider well the tracks over which the child should travel with profit and pleasure.") *Life* refers to academics presented as living thoughts and ideas rather than rote, dry facts. ("All the thought we offer to our children shall be living thought; no mere dry summaries of facts will do.")

The Charlotte Mason method is heavily based on literature. Workbooks and textbooks are rarely used. Many students use a Book of Centuries, which is a timeline kept in a notebook, and to which the student regularly adds as his or her understanding of history expands. Mason's philosophy emphasizes good penmanship and often the parent is instructed to dictate material for the child to practice writing. Journal writing is required. Aerobic exercise, including marching, gymnastics, and other floor exercises, are interspersed with academics, as are daily nature walks. Reading is an important activity but material that is *twaddle* is to be avoided. Instead, parents and children should read material that is *living*. What does that mean? According to Mason, "Here is another way to recognize a living book. First examine the book

---

[17]www.homeschool-curriculum-for-life.com/charlotte-mason-quotes.html

to see if it promotes noble thoughts rather than a jaded or misleading outlook on life." Anything else is, she says, "candy for the mind."[18]

The Mason method requires a lot of structure and dedication from the parent but, for many families, it is the perfect approach to home-schooling.

Further Resources on This Topic

Charlotte Mason Method
http://homeschooling.gomilpitas.com/methods/CharlotteMason.htm

Free e-book of the Charlotte Mason philosophy
http://simplycharlottemason.com/books/education-is/

39. What are Waldorf Schools?

Waldorf education addresses the child as no other education does. Learning, whether in chemistry, mathematics, history or geography, is imbued with life and so with joy, which is the only true basis for later study. The textures and colors of nature, the accomplishments and struggles of humankind fill the Waldorf students' imaginations and the pages of their beautiful books. Education grows into a union with life that serves them for decades.

—Rudolf Steiner College[19]

Waldorf schools got their start in 1919 with a man named Rudolf Steiner, an Austrian philosopher and teacher. Since then, the organiza-tion has expanded to more than 800 schools worldwide, with approxi-mately 150 of the schools located throughout the United States and Canada. (To locate a school in the United States, go to http://www.members.awsna.org/Public/SchoolListPage.aspx).

---

[18]http://bushnell.net/~peanuts/faq1.html
[19]http://www.steinercollege.edu/?q=node/132

The philosophy behind Waldorf schools is that children should be taught in a way that engages not just their heads but their hearts and hands as well. To this end, classes incorporate an arts-based curriculum that typically includes:

- music
- dance
- theatre
- writing
- literature
- legends and myths

Classrooms tend to be vividly painted and covered with student art-work. More emphasis is placed on lifelong learning and less on academic placement, competitive testing, and rewards for good behavior. Classes are also based less on grade levels than on the three developmental phases of childhood: 6 or 7 years, 7 to 14 years, and 14 to 18 years. It takes eight years to complete all three phases. The youngest phase emphasizes the use of storytelling, puppetry, singing, games, art, and cooking. The middle phase focuses on literature, history, science, math, foreign languages, PE, arts, and handwork. The oldest group studies

- humanities (history, literature, world cultures)
- science (physics, biology, chemistry, geology, math)
- arts and crafts (calligraphy, drawing, painting, pottery, sculpture, weaving)
- performing arts (orchestra, choir, drama)
- foreign languages
- physical education

Typically, students have the same teacher throughout all eight years of the program. Waldorf advocates believe this gives both teacher and student the opportunity to truly know and understand one another and develop a long-term relationship. What if the teacher and the student do not get along? One Waldorf site responds this way:

> *Waldorf class is something like a family. If a mother in a family does not get along with her son during a certain time, she does not consider resigning or replacing him with another child. Rather, she looks at the situation and sees what can be done to improve the relationship. In other words, the adult assumes responsibility and tries to change. This same approach is expected of the Waldorf teacher in a difficult situation. In almost every case she must ask herself: "How can I change so that the relationship becomes more positive?" One cannot expect this of the child. With the goodwill and active support of the parents, the teacher concerned can make the necessary changes and restore the relationship to a healthy and productive state.*[20]

Clearly, everything in the Waldorf philosophy can be applied to a homeschooling environment. You will have to use some creativity now and then—it is hard to have an orchestra with just you and your family—but everything is possible with a little effort and imagination.

Further Resources on This Topic

Rudolf Steiner School
www.steiner.edu
www.whywaldorfworks.org

40. What is a classical education philosophy?

Rigorous study develops virtue in the student. Aristotle defined virtue as the ability to act in accordance to what one knows to be right. The virtuous man (or woman) can force himself to do what he knows to be right, even when it runs against his inclinations. The classical education continually asks a student to work against his

---

[20]http://www.whywaldorfworks.org/02_W_Education/faq_about.asp

baser inclinations (laziness, or the desire to watch another half hour of TV) in order to reach a goal—mastery of a subject.
　　　　　—Susan Wise Bauer, "What is a Classical Education?"

A classical education is based on the three-part process of what advocates refer to as *training the mind*. The three put together are often called the *trivium*. According to Susan Wise Bauer, author of *The Well-Trained Mind*, students spend the earliest years on *absorbing facts*, the middle years on learning to *think through arguments*, and the high school years on learning to *express themselves*.

Stage 1: The Grammar Stage (grades 1 through 4)
Learning facts and focusing on the memorization rules of phonics, grammar, math, and so on.

Stage 2: The Logic Stage (grades 5 through 8)
Thinking more analytically, exploring cause and effect. This stage includes algebra, logic, analysis of texts, the scientific method.

Stage 3: The Rhetoric Stage (grades 9 through 12)
Learning to write and speak with *force and originality*. This stage includes art camps, college courses, foreign travel, apprenticeships, and the like.

Bauer goes on to explain,

A classical education, then, has two important aspects. It is language-focused. And it follows a specific three-part pattern: the mind must be first supplied with facts and images, then given the logical tools for organization of facts, and finally equipped to express conclusions. But that is not all. To the classical mind, all knowl-edge is interrelated. Astronomy (for example) is not studied in isolation; it's learned along with the history of scientific discovery, which leads into the church's relationship to science and from there to the intricacies of medieval church history. The reading of the Odyssey leads the student into the consideration of

Greek history, the nature of heroism, the development of the epic, and man's understanding of the divine.[21]

Those involved in this method of homeschooling generally suggest that a student's 12 years of school should center on three cycles of four historic eras:

- the Ancients
- the Middle Ages
- the Renaissance and Reformation
- modern times

Further Resources on This Topic

The well-trained mind
www.welltrainedmind.com

Classical education
http://homeschooling.gomilpitas.com/methods/Classical.htm

41. What about Montessori Schools?

We cannot know the consequences of suppressing a child's spontaneity when he is just beginning to be active. We may even suffocate life itself. That humanity which is revealed in all its intellectual splendor during the sweet and tender age of childhood should be respected with a kind of religious veneration. It is like the sun which appears at dawn or a flower just beginning to bloom. Education cannot be effective unless it helps a child to open up himself to life.

—Maria Montessori

---

[21]http://capmag.com/article.asp?ID=286

The beginnings of the Montessori method can be traced to 1907 and Dr. Maria Montessori, the first woman in Italy to become a physician. Through her observations of child development, she created her own *casa dei bambini,* or children's house, in Rome. Today, there are more than 4,000 certified Montessori schools throughout the United States and 7,000 worldwide. The method is also used in countless home-schools throughout the country.

The philosophy behind Montessori is that it emphasizes learning through all five senses, and learning at a child's pace. Other key elements include the following:

- Classes place children into three-year age groups (3–6, 6–9, 9–12, and so on). Child-to-child teaching and socialization are encouraged and there is constant interaction in the classroom.
- Classrooms feature work centers based on subject area. Children are free to move from one center to another rather than remain in their desks, and they are permitted to stay at any one center as long as they wish.
- Papers are not graded and corrected but discussed.
- There are no grades or other forms of reward and punishment. Assessment is typically done through a portfolio. Children's success in any grade is based on how happy and mature he or she is and how much they love learning.
- Character education is often a part of the daily lessons.
- Students often design contracts with their teachers to determine what will be accomplished during the course of the year.

Further Resources on This Topic

Free downloads, video clips and more about the Montessori method
http://www.michaelolaf.net/

List of Montessori schools by area
http://www.montessori.edu/refs.html

42. What does the press report about homeschooling?

Reporters and their editors are humans, and may make mistakes (just like the rest of us). Inaccurate statements or information often appear in articles due to ignorance, innocent misunderstandings, or the stresses of working under tight deadlines. Most reporters are not familiar with homeschooling, and their reporting may be influenced unconsciously by their own public school experiences or by popular misconceptions about homeschooling.

—Celeste Land, "Talking about Homeschooling with the Media"[22]

It seems as though every few weeks another homeschooling story pops up in a newspaper or a magazine. Many times it is a great story that shows homeschooling families doing what they want to be doing—living and teaching and growing. Many of the articles include the obligatory comment from the local school district, the state DOE, or some other public school advocate—but that is to be expected.

Occasionally there will be a horrific news story about some mentally ill person who has done something violent. If the person happens to be homeschooled, that fact is emphasized for some reason: *Homeschooled Mother Goes Berserk* or *Family of Five Homeschoolers Committing Arson*. By contrast, no headline reads, *Public Schooled Man Steals Priceless Art* or *Public Schooled Hackers Strike Again*. This kind of bias, of course, makes it appear as if home education played a part in the crime—which is rarely (if ever) true. We can only hope that, in time, the media will begin to present homeschooling as just another educational alternative, equal to the others.

Further Resources on This Topic

"Homeschooling in the United States: 2003," National Center for Education Statistics
http://nces.ed.gov/pubs2006/homeschool/

---

[22]http://www.vahomeschoolers.org/pdf/hsing_and_media.pdf

News and Commentary
http://www.homeedmag.com/newscomm/

HSLDA (Home School Legal Defense Association) News Archives
http://www.hslda.org/inthenewsarchive.asp

43. What role can grandparents play in homeschooling?

All across the country, grandparents are successfully taking the lead in homeschooling their grandchildren. They are finding that this unique opportunity enables them to fulfill their own needs to stay active while it also helps provide a valuable service to the youngsters in their lives.

—"Grandparents Can Take the Lead
in Homeschooling Children"[23]

If your parents (your children's grandparents) are not yet on board with your homeschooling decision (or even if they are), give some thought to involving them in your routine. If they live nearby they can place an active role by

- teaching material you do not know
- teaching about your family history
- teaching old-fashioned skills
- helping with childcare
- reading out loud
- playing games
- telling stories (real and pretend)

---

[23]http://www.articlesbase.com/education-articles/grandparents-can-take-the-lead-in-homeschooling-children-901568.html

If grandparents live too far away to help out easily, you can involve them by asking them to

- write letters to your children
- call your children and ask them what they have learned
- send educational materials (such as magazine subscriptions and zoo or museum memberships)
- be supportive of homeschooling

Being involved often helps grandparents feel needed; it also lets them better understand how homeschooling works. In a growing number of households, grandparents are even themselves taking over the role of homeschooling.

Further Resources on This Topic

"Homeschoolers Need Grandparents (and Grandparents Need Grandchildren)," by Linda Schrock Taylor
http://www.lewrockwell.com/taylor/taylor84.html

"May a Grandmother Homeschool?" by Ann Zeise
http://homeschooling.gomilpitas.com/articles/080107.htm

Where

THIS SECTION WILL explore where to find the resources, materials, people, and answers that you need to homeschool. Clearly, where you live will have a huge impact on some of these questions. Those living in a large city, for example, will be able to find a teacher's supply store and places to go on field trips more easily than those who live out in the country and have to drive an hour even to get to a grocery store. The Internet has done wonders to equalize this situation, however, and almost anything you need can be found if you just know where to look, and have a credit card handy!

Home, Home All the Day (sung to the tune of) *Home on the Range*

(1) Oh, give me the day, with no soccer to play, and no doctor's appointments to meet,

But let me stay home and take care of my own, and my life will
be peaceful and sweet.

CHORUS

Home, Home all the day,
Where the children study and play,
Where seldom is heard, the hurry up word,
And the van's in the carport all day!

(2) Oh give me a morn, where no shoes must be worn, for the kid-
dos have no place to be;
and the Mom mustn't meet; oh, that day would be sweet! And
would be such a blessing to me!

(3) Oh give me the days where we all wear P.J.s and the studies do
not start until ten.
Where we snuggle with books or we learn to be cooks and little
voices beg *Do it again!*

(4) Oh give me a place with a smile on each face, where we finger-
paint lions and bears.
No one says, *What a mess!* We just feel very blessed for the
moment when everyone shares!

(5) Oh, give me the hours where we study wildflowers and wonder
at the sight of the bees.
Where science is fun in the afternoon sun and our lunchroom is
under the trees.

(6) Oh, give me a day with no packed lunches to make
and no tears and the stomach ache fake.
Oh let me stay home, though it might take a loan
and the dishes and laundry can wait.

(Chorus and verse 1 by Marji McIlvaine, verse 2 by Dalene Barnes, verses 3–5
by M. Praze (with help from children!), and verse 6 by Peggy in Arizona)
http://homeschooling.gomilpitas.com/humor/118.htm

44. Where can I find homeschooling curricula and other materials?

Your children did not come in a package . . . why should their learning materials?

　　　　　　　　　　　　　　—Susan, homeschooling mom

Just as no two families homeschool are the same, no two families will need the same materials and supplies. There are too many variables. For instance, how old is your child? Clearly you will need different of curricula for the primary grades than for the secondary ones. Second, what type of homeschooling are you pursuing? The more formal and school-like it is, the more materials you will need to have on hand. Some families purchase entire curricula from companies, while others put theirs together from here and there. Next, ask yourself what you already have on hand from school, from your own education, from gifts, and from other sources. You may discover you have more than you think when you gather it all in one place. Finally, ask your children what kind of materials they would like you to have. Do they love workbooks to write in or experiments to try? Based on their personalities and traits, what kinds of materials would best suit them?

Once you have answered these questions, you can start looking for the supplies you want. Before you purchase anything, though, try asking other homeschoolers whether they use the material. Ask for their opinion: what worked and what did not, what they liked and what they did not. If possible, ask to borrow the material and use it with your kids for a little while, or see if you can get any of the books through your public library. See how your kids—and you—like the material. Do they think it fits you and your learning styles and homeschooling philosophy? If not, you should wait until you find the material that is just right among the many different products on the market. Doing your research before pulling out your wallet can definitely save you money as well as disappointment.

Homeschooling materials can be found at little or no cost in a number of places, including

- teacher's supply stores
- department stores
- office supply stores
- online stores
- garage sales
- curriculum swaps
- thrift stores
- other homeschoolers
- homeschooling conferences
- craigslist

Many homeschooling materials can also be found through your local library so they are essentially free. You can ask for an educator's library card, which will allow you to keep materials much longer than the traditional card. Other sources of materials include swapping with other homeschoolers and, of course, creating your own.

The Internet has countless sites offering free curriculum as well, from math practice pages to maps to spelling tests. Try typing in anything from *free homeschooling materials* to *free worksheets*, and you will find hundreds of choices. Surfing the Net can often garner enough information to make up your own unit studies and practice sheets.

Just remember one important part of finding your curriculum—it is *not* required for homeschooling. Almost everything you tackle, especially in the youngest grades, can be done with what you have at home and can find at the library. Do not feel that you have to purchase something, at least not in the beginning. Just start and see what is missing—if anything.

Further Resources on This Topic

Materials for homeschooling
http://www.homeschoolingbooks.com/

Resources for homeschooling

http://www.midnightbeach.com/hs/

http://www.homeschoolersofmaine.org/free_curriculum_on_internet
.htm

http://www.letshomeschool.com/articles10.html

45. Where can I find local support?

Homeschooling and public schooling are as opposite as two sides of a coin. In a homeschooling environment, the teacher need not be certified, but the child must *learn. In a public school environment, the teacher* must *be certified, but the child need* not *learn.*

—Gene Royer

Local homeschooling support groups can be found in local newspapers, libraries, teacher's supply stores, and local store and church bulletin boards. An earlier section outlined how to create your own support group if you cannot find one or if the one in your area does not fit your needs.

One of the best ways to find a local group is to ask every homeschooler you meet. Local groups are great because they can point you to the best resources in your area, help you connect with families in your neighborhood, and share materials with you. These support groups often are the avenue through which you will meet other families and your children will make friends to play or socialize with.

Further Resources on This Topic

Local homeschooling support group locator
http://localhs.com/

Advice on establishing your own local support group
http://www.suite101.com/blog/roserighter/create_a_local_support_
group

46. Where can I find state support?

Earth and sky, woods and fields, lakes and rivers, the mountain and the sea, are excellent schoolmasters, and teach some of us more than we can ever learn from books.

—John Lubbock

State-by-state homeschooling support groups can be found in the back of this book as well as on the Internet. You can find them at additional sources and since there tends to be relatively high turnover in contact information, it is best to check several different sources to find the one that is most up to date.

Support groups are helpful because they are aware of specific issues and cases surrounding the laws of your particular state, as well as resources and opportunities available to you.

Further Resources on This Topic

State-by-state support group lists
http://homeschooling.about.com/od/supportgroupsbystate/a/
   sgusa.htm
http://www.learning4liferesources.com/homeschool_page2.html

47. Where can I find national support?

If a man does not keep pace with his companions, perhaps it is because he hears a different drummer. Let him step to the music which he hears, however measured or far away.

—Henry David Thoreau

A list of national resources can be found in the back of this book. Many of the national groups have some sort of philosophy or theme around which they are centered (such as a specific type of homeschooling). Make sure to read their mission statement or purpose to see whether it matches your perspective.

Further Resources on This Topic

Links to national organizations
http://www.homeschoolcentral.com/hsorg.htm

National Home Education Research Institute
www.nheri.org/

48. Where do my other children go when I am homeschooling?

Learning theory tells us to teach children as individuals who learn in their own unique manner. The finest possible curriculum is precisely the one that starts with each child's singular means of learning. Instruction and guidance are best provided by those with an intimate understanding of the individual child and a deep commitment to the child's education. These principles derive not merely from the homeschooling movement but from contemporary research into how children learn. They are not merely adages fabricated by homeschoolers but precepts grounded in a science that should inspire us to reconsider both our roles as parents and the shape of public education.

—David Guterson

The answer to this mainly depends on how many children you have and what age they are. The majority of homeschooling families have several children, so this is a familiar problem.

If the children are quite young, you could give them some games, toys, crayons, and other arts and crafts supplies to play with at the table while you work with your older children. Most of the time they will want to be where you are and involved as much as possible, and just sharing books and pens and paper with their siblings is frequently enough to keep them content. You might be amazed at how much they are learning just by being there!

You can wait to do one-on-one work with your homeschooler until the littler ones are nursing, watching a movie or show, taking a nap, or going to bed for the night. You might also hire a teenage homeschooler or ask a grandparent to come over and watch your youngest ones for a couple of hours each day so you can focus on lessons. In most cases, older children will be in school themselves. Or, if you are homeschooling after school hours, you can suggest they work on homework or just listen in while you homeschool. You might even consider asking your older children to help teach your younger ones.

Keep in mind two of homeschooling's biggest benefits: you can choose when to do it (so you can schedule around nap times, for example) and it does not take nearly as many hours as public school does.

Further Resources on This Topic

Homeschooling multiple-aged children
http://www.associatedcontent.com/article/92729/how_to_
    homeschool_multiple_grades_and.html?cat=25

Games, arts, and crafts for younger children
http://www.enchantedlearning.com/crafts/toddler/

49. Where can I go on field trips?

Knowledge which is acquired under compulsion has no hold on the mind. Therefore, do not use compulsion, but let early education be rather a sort of amusement; this will better enable you to find out the natural bent of the child.

—Plato

Field trips are almost always a high point in public school—and they can be just as much fun, not to mention far more diverse and frequent, in homeschooling. There are the usual places, like zoos and museums, but look beyond that—there are countless places within the community that can be fascinating to visit and walk through. Since you are not tied to a school's schedule, you also have far more leeway in where you can go or how long you can stay. For example, if a national monument is a half day's travel from your home, you can visit it, spend the night, and return the following day (all without even having to fill out a permission slip!). You can go on a weekday, when places like these tend to be less crowded.

Here are 40 possible places to consider for field trips:

1. art gallery
2. historic village
3. theatre production
4. factory
5. bakery
6. farm
7. Native American reservation
8. monument
9. festival or fair
10. historic landmark
11. aquarium
12. animal shelter
13. park
14. symphony hall
15. planetarium
16. courthouse
17. orchard
18. television station
19. newspaper office
20. radio station
21. water treatment plant
22. restaurant
23. power plant
24. science center
25. state or city capitol building
26. railroad station
27. wildlife center
28. amusement park
29. college campus
30. camp
31. fish hatchery
32. garden
33. farmers market
34. fire station or police station
35. pumpkin patch
36. nursing home
37. post office
38. rock quarry
39. airport
40. greenhouse or nursery

In planning a field trip, you will need to consider several details.

1. How many are going—just you and your family or your entire support group? If multiple families are going, have a sign-up sheet so you have a good idea of numbers.
2. How long do you plan to stay?

3. Are there any costs involved? If so, how much? Be sure to ask if discounts are offered for educators.

4. How long will it take to get there and back?

5. Have you called first and made arrangements or reservations? *This is very important.* Ask what rules they have about numbers and ages too. Get directions, details about parking, and any other helpful information.

6. Do you know what you want your children to learn from the experience? What educational activities can you tie in to the trip? Do you want to cover any material before the trip? during? after? Be sure not to focus too much on this angle—you want your kids to have fun first and then learning naturally follows. (Just ask Aristotle!)

Further Resources on This Topic

Field trip links from A to Z Home's Cool
http://homeschooling.gomilpitas.com/trips/FieldTrips.htm.

Field trip suggestions by subject area
http://www.letshomeschool.com/articles60.html

Downloadable field trip form full of ideas and educational activities
http://www.oklahomahomeschool.com/pdf%20documents/
   Field%20Trip%20Planning%20Guide.pdf

50. Where should I set up the schoolroom?

In general, the best teacher or caregiver cannot match a parent of even ordinary education and experience.

—Dr. Raymond Moore

First, ask yourself if you are sure you have to set up a schoolroom at all. Really—stop and explore the reason behind this. Almost every possible type of homeschooling activity can be done sitting at the kitchen table or on the floor in the playroom or the living room. Desks and chairs are straight out of the public school model and are not necessary.

It is entirely possible, however, that having a separate schoolroom is simply what you and/or your children *want*. Perhaps you like having it away from other rooms and the distractions they include. Maybe your son or daughter likes the feeling of being in school or just finds the desk a comfortable or familiar place to work. Chances are that you will eventually discard that desk, but many families feel good starting there.

In that case, where can you set one up?

Walk through your house and see if there are any underused rooms. Is there a room that is full of stuff you are not using? Perhaps you set up a sewing room but rarely ever utilize it. Maybe you have a room with exercise equipment or boxes of storage materials. Is there an extra bedroom used for guests—but rarely? Each of these might work well once you do some rearranging and reorganizing. You might also consider the attic, the basement, large closets, or the garage.

If you do not have any possible rooms like this, walk through your house again, this time considering how you might move furniture around to set a up corner for homeschooling materials. Remember that you will want this room to be comfortable for you as well as the kids since you will be spending time there. If possible, it should be big enough for a filing cabinet (for papers, and the like), shelves (for games, books, and other materials) and outlets for lights and a computer or laptop. You might want to put up maps or posters on the wall. Some families put up the multiplication tables, calendars, timelines, or other educational materials. Save space for your children's artwork and craft projects. Do not think you have to make the area look *school-ish*, however. This is your house, your style, your preferences, and your homeschooling. Decorate it in whatever way you and your kids envision! Regardless of how it looks when you start homeschooling, a year or two later, it will very likely look entirely different.

Further Resources on This Topic

Tips for organizing a school area

http://homeschooling.about.com/cs/gettingstarted/a/backschool area.htm

Creating a homeschool room
http://www.associatedcontent.com/article/101616/how_to_
create_a_homeschool_room_in.html?cat=30

51. Where can my teen find an internship, apprenticeship, or similar program?

For me, home education has been a terrific journey away from static forms of learning, institutional hoops to jump through, forms to please others, and a journey into a magical world of wonder and discovery. Not relaxing, but certainly an exciting process.

—Val, homeschooling mom

One of the best ways for your older children to learn more about a particular job or profession is through an internship or apprenticeship. Typically this is an unpaid position but it teaches young people the basics of what is involved in a certain career and can help them pinpoint what they do (and definitely do *not*) want to do in the future. It teaches new skills, helps teens network with people, and looks great on a resume. In addition, internships get your child's foot in the door with a company, increasing the likelihood of getting a real job there later down the road.

Sit down with your teens and talk about their interests. What field do they see themselves working in? What are their favorite hobbies? What are their strongest skills? Brainstorm what kinds of jobs could come from the answers to these questions. Are they interested in music? How about working in a music school? a store that sells instruments, repairs broken ones, or restores them? a radio station? a recording studio? a CD store? Perhaps they have an interest in social work. How about a day-care center? a nursing home? a homeless shelter? Are they fascinated by criminal justice and related fields? How about working with Search and Rescue, the Police Cadet Program, or the state's Liquor Commission Control (teens work as decoys to make sure businesses are following state-mandated age requirements).

An online and/or book search of internships available can sometimes be frustrating, since mostly you will find summer opportunities. This makes sense: most teens are only available for this kind of work in the summertime when school is out. For the homeschooler, though, any time of the year is workable. If you wait until the summer, competition for each position can be fierce. What can be done instead? Here are some options.

1. Get in touch with the places that offer summer internships and ask if they would be open to hosting your teen during other seasons of the year. Often companies are not even aware that someone might be interested and available during other months. Asking costs you nothing and could gain everything.
2. Look around your community and see what it has to offer in the fields that interest your teen. If he wants to know more about animal care, call your closest vet and/or animal shelter. If she is interested in publishing, see if there is a local newspaper office or printing house. Just because an organization does not advertise an internship does not mean it is not willing to offer one.
3. Be sure to look beyond your immediate community. There might be more opportunities in larger cities, so explore those as well. Your teen might be able to use public transportation, or the help of a friend or relative, to get there and back. Be creative!

When you contact any of these places be ready to explain the reasons your child is interested in an internship, as well as the different ways he or she could benefit the company or organization. (Here is your chance to brag a little!) It would not be surprising to find that the place you are contacting has never offered any kind of program like this before. If you sell the idea well enough, you may be creating a new opportunity for countless other young people in your community.

If your son or daughter is able to land a local (or regional) internship, it is important that they take it as seriously as they would paid employment. If they are scheduled to work, they should be there, on time, dressed appropriately. Behavior should be professional. This is an opportunity for everyone—the business or organization, the community, and your teen—to benefit.

Further Resources on This Topic

State-by-state listing of internship and volunteer jobs
http://www.groovejob.com/browse/internships/

Current opportunities for internships are listed in the latest edition
   of *The Internship Bible* published by the Princeton Review.

52. Where can my child learn how to play an instrument or join a band or an orchestra?

Education is not the filling of a pail, but the lighting of a fire.
                                                    —William Butler Yeats

It is easy to fall into thinking that the only way your child can learn anything, a subject, a skill, a topic, is through public school. After all, that is the model that most generations today know best. However, at one time, all skills and materials a child needed to know were taught at home. That can still be true as long as parents realize they do not have to teach everything themselves—that is what the rest of the community, and the Internet, are for!

If your child wants to learn how to play an instrument and play in a band or an orchestra or sing and be in a choir, those things are still quite possible without school. Here are a dozen possibilities to explore:

1. Do you or your partner play an instrument or sing? If so, share your skills. Drag out the guitar, dust off the piano, and warm up the vocal cords.

2. Does anyone else in your family have these skills? Siblings, aunts, uncles, cousins? Talk to them about lessons. Can't afford lessons? What can you barter in return?

3. Do you have a friend or neighbor who has these skills? See above!

4. Check the telephone book or online to see who gives lessons in your community.

5. Ask your local school district whether your child can enroll only for band or orchestra or choir. (Watch for red tape and clauses that may surprise you.)

6. Check out the bulletin boards in local music stores. This is a great place for people to post their ads. Ask the owners (often musicians themselves) whether they can recommend a teacher.

7. Go to the library or online and find how-to videos. Rent or buy them and see how much they can teach you about an instrument.

8. Ask your support group whether anyone (including other homeschooling kids) teaches these skills.

9. If your support group is large, consider creating a homeschooling band or orchestra or choir with the kids in your group. It has been done many times. (Think Jonas Brothers!)

10. Check to see if there are any music camps in your area (usually summer camps) that teach music and instruments.

11. Find out if your city has a symphony orchestra and ask if you can sit in and listen to rehearsals. While there, inquire as to how to find lessons.

12. Community choirs are found in almost all cities. Churches often offer great opportunities to sing. Check with them, as well as with your YM/YWCA, chamber of commerce, and online city listings.

As you can see from this initial list, if your child wants to pursue music, there are many different avenues to explore. And guess what? You have the time to do so!

Further Resources on This Topic

Homeschooling and music
http://homeschooling.gomilpitas.com/explore/homemademusic.htm

53. *Where can my child learn sports or join a team?*

The founding fathers in their wisdom decided that children were an unnatural strain on parents, so they provided jails called schools, equipped with tortures called education. School is where you go between when your parents can't take you and industry can't take you.

—John Updike

Playing sports builds muscles and supports good health. It teaches a love for physical activity. It often encourages teamwork, cooperation, and discipline. Depending on your point of view, it illustrates sportsmanship and introduces healthy competition or encourages judgment (grading) and uncomfortable peer competition.

Public school is only one avenue for a child who is interested in athletics. Here are some ways a homeschooled child can get involved:

1. Start easy. Are you or your partner skilled at a particular sport? Share your experience and talent with your kids.
2. Neighborhood games. Check and see whether other children in your neighborhood would like to get together on a regular basis and play basketball, baseball, football, or whatever sport you choose.
3. Join the YW/YMCA. These organizatons offer a wide range of sports programs for all ages, as well as sports camps.
4. Check with your local school district; they sometimes allow homeschoolers to join their sports teams.
5. Explore your local parks and recreation programs; they typically offer free or low-cost classes.
6. Check with your friends, relatives, neighbors, and coworkers to see if they have skills in a particular sport that they would be willing to teach your children. Does Uncle Bob know how to play golf? Is cousin Jane a great tennis player?
7. Ask around your local support group for possible teams or teachers. If your group is large enough, why not form your own teams to play against other regional homeschoolers?

8. Check the phone book or online to see whether there are local coaches who give individual lessons.

Finding a way for your son or daughter to join a team or learn a sport is not difficult. It means making the effort to look at your family, community, neighborhood, and city to see what it might have to offer that you never realized before.

Further Resources on This Topic

The Home School Athletic Association
www.hsaa.org

Home School Sports Net (HSPN)
www.hspn.net

Find Sports Now
www.findsportsnow.com

54. Where can my child get physical education (PE)?

The idea is to educate, not follow anyone's schedule about when something should be studied.

—Ray Drouillard

Much of the answer to this question can be found in the preceding pages. Not every child loves physical education enough, however, to want to pursue a specific sport or join a team. Instead, they just want—or more likely you and your partner want—to make sure that exercise is part of your regular homeschool program.

In this case, the key to making PE work for you and your family is to make it fun. Skip PE class and play games instead. If your kids perceive running around as work instead of part of playing tag or hide-and-seek or a fun soccer game in the backyard, they are more apt to complain and not want to move away from their favorite video game system.

Second, since today's generation is geared so strongly to high-tech gadgets, consider integrating PE and electronics through games such as

Dance Dance Revolution (available for Xbox, Wii, Playstation 2 and 3, and computer), Just Dance (Wii), and Wii Fit. Kids often relate well to exercise when it is connected to game playing.

Next, look at PE, not as a class but as a way of life for the entire family. Instead of building time into your schedule for PE class, build in time for a family bike ride, swim at the pool, walk around the Y track, or other activities. Everyone needs exercise, and by participating yourself you are setting the right role model as well.

Finally, talk to your kids about what kind of exercise they would like to pursue. Maybe your teenage son wants to lift weights. Your daughter might be interested in gymnastics. Find out what appeals to them and then see what you can find in your area regarding clubs, lessons, and groups.

Further Resources on This Topic

Homeschooling PE

http://homeschoolingpe.com/

http://www.thehomeschoolmom.com/schoolroom/physed.php

55. Where can my teenager find someone to date?

The immediate case against compulsory school for adolescents is quite simply their barbarity: it is a triangle of hatred, humiliation, and contempt.

—Frank Musgrove

Walk in the shoes of a teen today and you will quickly find out that they encounter people near their ages in places other than school. By not sending them to public school, you will not doom your children to a solitary life. In fact, once you begin homeschooling, your kids will often find more opportunities to meet people than they ever did because they have so much more time not spent sitting inside school.

Where can teens find someone to date? How about:

- part-time jobs
- volunteer activities
- clubs or groups (Boy/Girl Scouts, 4H, and so on)
- parties
- malls
- neighbors' houses
- friends' houses
- other homeschoolers

These are just a few possible ideas. Your teens will meet peers wherever they tend to go. Often large homeschooling support groups will organize events specifically for the teens, such as dances, movie outings, bowling, and other fun activities to facilitate teen interaction. If they do not do so, that might be enough inspiration for you to give it a try.

Further Resources on This Topic

Safe online connections chat rooms
www.teenhomeschoolhang.com
www.homeschoolchristian.com/Chat/TeenChat.html

56. Where can I find guidance on how to design my curriculum?

The newer and broader picture suggests that the child emerges into literacy by actively speaking, reading, and writing in the context of real life, not through filling out phonics worksheets or memorizing words.

—Charlotte Mason

Whether you plan to buy a complete, packaged curriculum or to put one together from scratch, you will want to get some advice or guidance first. Where can you get it? Here are some possibilities:

- **The company that produced the materials.** Granted, they will be a bit prejudiced, but you can find out a great deal about the product (and even get a few free samples) if you write or email and ask questions.
- **Other homeschoolers.** They will have great advice for you on many products and can often point out where to find less expensive materials or other ways to save money.
- **Your children.** Before you spend money on any supplies or materials, show them to your kids. Do they show an interest? If not, think twice. There are many ways to teach every subject, so do not feel you have to use a workbook or flash cards. You can use whatever works best for your child.
- **Go online.** Many homeschoolers post comments and reviews of products on their blogs and forums. In the search box, type the name of the product you are considering and then reviews.
- **Store clerks.** If you go to a teacher's supply store, ask the people working there what seems to be selling the best or is the most popular.

The more information you have before you spend any money, the stronger the chance that you will get material that you and your children can use rather than something to shove under the short leg of the dining room table.

Further Resources on This Topic

Links to homeschooling products
http://www.home-school.com/catalog/
http://www.homeschoolsupercenter.com/new_site/home.php

Home Schooling on a Shoe String, by Melissa Morgan and Judith Waite Allee, has valuable information on making your own curriculum or finding it at low cost.

57. Where can I buy a complete curriculum—and should I do so?

We should spend less time ranking children and more time helping them identify their natural competencies and gifts, and cultivate those. There are hundreds and hundreds of ways to succeed and many, many different abilities that will help you get there.

—Howard Gardner

Where to get a curriculum is easy; deciding whether or not you need one is not. The answer to this question is complex and will require that you figure out your homeschooling philosophy, at least in part. The more structured you are, the more likely you will purchase a packaged curriculum. Remember the continuum mentioned earlier in this book? On one end was schooling at home, and on the other was unschooling. As a general rule, the closer you are to schooling at home, the more apt you are to buy a set curriculum from one of the many companies who offer them. Another general rule? You will never again spend as much on curriculum as you do the first year. Part of the trial-and-error process is trying products and either incorporating them or rejecting them. Experimenting with different materials is natural and fine—but it can be costly and should be done carefully.

If you have decided to start with a curriculum and you have already sought others' advice on what to get, where can you find one? The two easiest places are online and at teacher's supply stores. There are many websites that sell entire packages and of course, a number of teacher's supply stores do too. Such packages can run into several hundreds of dollars, especially if you are buying packages for multiple grade levels, so doing your research first is wise.

Further Resources on This Topic

Packaged curriculum
www.learningthings.com/articles/
    www.core-curriculum.com

Review of several types of packaged curriculum
http://school.familyeducation.com/home-schooling/
    curriculum-planning/38847.html?page=2

When

MANY HOMESCHOOLING PARENTS have multiple questions about timing. When to start and stop? When to move from one grade to another? When to start the day and end it? When to break for the summer—or not? This section answers those questions and makes it clear, once again, that the *when* issues (like all the other sections) are *entirely up to you, your partner, and your children.* You are in control and you get to make the decisions. This statement will be repeated again and again, because it is the truth. One of the best parts of homeschooling is that you are at the helm, you make the decisions, and you design it to fit you, your partner, and your kids. Isn't that amazing freedom?

The Top 10 Advantages to Homeschooling

10. Your kids never tell you that you are a lot dumber than their teacher.

9. Cleaning out the refrigerator can double as chemistry lab.

8. You can post the Ten Commandments on your school room wall and will not get sued.

7. You never have to drive your child's forgotten lunch to school.

6. If you get caught talking to yourself, you can claim you are having a PTA meeting.

5. The only debate about the school lunch program is whose turn it is to cook.

4. You never have to face the dilemma of whether to take your child's side or the teacher's side in a dispute at school.

3. If your child gets drugs at school, it is probably Tylenol.

2. If your child claims that the dog ate his homework, you can ask the dog.

1. Some day your children will consider you to be a miracle-working expert and will turn to you for advice.[1]

58. When during the year should I start and stop homeschooling?

School days, I believe, are the unhappiest in the whole span of human existence. They are full of dull, unintelligible tasks, new and unpleasant ordinances, brutal violations of common sense and common decency. It does not take a reasonably bright boy long to discover that most of what is rammed into him is nonsense, and that no one really cares very much whether he learns it or not.

—H.L. Mencken

By the time you finish this book, you may be tired of the following sentence but you will probably also have integrated the concept. *There is no right way to homeschool.* Every time you come up against a question like this one, the response is a simple *it is up to you.* What month you begin homeschooling, as well as what month you stop, is entirely, completely,

---

[1]Adapted from A to Z Home's Cool, http://homeschooling.gomilpitas.com/humor/131.htm/

and utterly up to you, your partner, and your children. Just because public school starts in August or September and lets out in May or June does not mean you have to. You can start and stop whenever you want. You can take breaks whenever you want, not when the calendar dictates. If you take your child out of school in November, you can start home-schooling then—or wait a month or two. If you are not done in June, keep going. You can go year round—or not. It is up to you.

Further Resources on This Topic

Example of and anecdotes about homeschooling
http://homeschooling.about.com/od/scheduling/a/dailyschedule
.htm

Homeschooling assignment sheets to download for free
http://homeschooling.about.com/gi/o.htm?zi=1/XJ/Ya&zTi=1&
sdn=homeschooling&cdn=education&tm=7&gps=272_195_
1020_505&f=22&tt=14&bt=0&bts=1&zu=http%3A//www
.studysystemizer.com/freestuff/todo.htm

59. When is summer break?

Parents give up their rights when they drop the children off at public school.

—Melina Harmon, U.S. Federal Judge

You are probably shaking your head right about now because you know what the answer is to this question (unless you flipped right to this one without reading the rest first). Summer break is whenever you want it to be. It does not even have to be in summer; it can even be in another season. It can be weeks or months long. It can even be nonex-istent if you go year round. The public school model is nothing but a model and not one that you have to follow for any reason. Take a break when it feels right.

Should you go year round? That is (yes, again!) up to you and your partner and children. Those who think it is a good idea often cite a number of logical reasons such as less need to spend time reviewing, more school days to fill up with fun events like field trips, more time to get material covered, and more frequent, shorter breaks instead of one long one in the middle of the year. Those against it also have logical reasons such as kids needing a break—especially at this time of year when the weather is nice and there are more opportunities for fun events, internships, and trips. Both sides of the argument have merit, so think about it, weigh the two sides and then see what makes most sense to you and all involved.

Further Resources on This Topic

Pros and cons of homeschooling through the summer break
http://school.familyeducation.com/home-schooling/educational
  -philosophy/38366.html

Summer break and homeschooling
http://www.suite101.com/reference/summer_break

60. When do we register with the public school or the state?

The idea of learning acceptable social skills in a school is as absurd to me as learning nutrition from a grocery store.

—Lisa Russell

When (and whether) you have to register with your state when you choose to homeschool depends on the laws of your particular state, as well as if you are removing your child from school or if you are just starting with a child who has never been enrolled in any public school system.

Not all states require a letter of intent, although the majority do. These letters protect your child from being considered truant and inform the school district that it is not officially responsible for the education of your child. That letter is due, typically, by the child's eighth birthday (which means you can try homeschooling for several years before you have to announce it) but again, check with your state laws. Some states also require that you submit this letter every year.

If you are withdrawing your child from school, as mentioned in Section 3, Question 28, you need to submit some type of letter so that the school knows your child is not just suddenly absent but is pursuing alternative forms of education. The letter is usually submitted to the superintendent of the district.

What goes into a letter of intent? You simply say that you have chosen to homeschool, and give your children's names and ages and your signature. Many states have a form you can fill out. It is essential that you know that this is the *only* information you are legally required to provide. Anything asked beyond that is *optional*. You do not have to provide details about curriculum or anything else.

If you have any questions about how to fill out the form, where to send it, what to include and not include, and even whether you have to do it or not, ask other homeschoolers. They will often have great advice for you.

Further Resources on This Topic

Sample letter of intent
http://www.christianhomeschoolers.com/hs_letter.html

61. When do we give our children standardized tests?

You will not reap the fruit of individuality in your children if you clone their education.

—Marilyn Howshall

Do your children have to take national standardized tests such as the ACT or the SAT? Once again, it depends on where you live. Some states require that your homeschooled children be tested at certain grade levels (typically third, fifth, eighth, and tenth); others do not. If you live in one that does not, you may skip to the next question because this one does not concern you. If, however, you live in one that does require these tests, read on.

Some homeschoolers have to take their children to a testing center or hire a certified tester to come to their house and administer the test. Sometimes it can be done with an individual family; other times it might be given to an entire group (like your support group) at a time. In some states, parents are allowed to administer the test themselves. In recent years, another option has been to order an online testing program which is timed and completed on the Internet. No matter what form of testing you choose, there will be a cost involved, typically about $35 per test, depending on the age of your children.

If you have been homeschooling your children from the beginning, they may have very little experience with standardized tests. You can help them prepare by providing sample tests (found online). Find ways to ease test anxiety.

Once your children have had the test, what then? It gets a little tricky. In many states, you are required to administer the test but are not asked to turn in the score. If you are not asked, you are not required to do so. If you *are* asked, then you turn it in. Typically, as long as your child scored above the bottom fifteenth percentile, you are okay. If not, the public school may put some pressure on you to bring up the score. (This virtually never happens.)

Some homeschoolers really appreciate what they learn from having their children tested and are happy to cooperate with the state laws. They use the scores as feedback about their children's strengths and weaknesses, and adjust their curriculum accordingly. Others have their doubts about how accurately these test scores reflect children's knowledge, and do what they can to avoid having their children take them. They feel it is intrusive and ineffective. Whether or not to have your children tested is an issue that you will have to study and decide on—depending on what your state laws require.

Further Resources on This Topic

Why some homeschoolers are against mandatory testing
http://www.terriebittner.com/everythingelse/standardizedtests.html

Overview of the testing process and other details
http://www.homeschool-curriculum-savings.com/homeschool
-testing.html

62. When will my child learn how to _____?

Education is an admirable thing, but it is well to remember from time to time that nothing worth knowing can be taught.

—Oscar Wilde

The reason we left a blank at the end of this question is because each family has its own specific concerns. What if he never learns the multiplication tables? What if she never learns to read? What if he never learns to stop fidgeting when we homeschool? What if she never learns to get up before noon? The questions change from one family to another, so to give one blanket answer is difficult.

As you ponder this question (usually at 3 A.M. when it seems like the world's problems all rest on your shoulders), there are several things to keep in mind. The first one is to extrapolate: what if he never does learn the skill you are concerned about? Often you focus on the question and never take it much further than to think, Oh, that would be bad! (A little like crossing the streams in the movie *Ghostbusters*.) But *would it really*? It depends on the skill. If it is reading, for example, yes; if your child does not learn it, that could create problems. It would not be the end of the world, but it could cause difficulties in many realms. On the other hand, if your child does not learn the capitals of every state in the country, will tragedy befall anyone? No. What if he does not learn the definition of *dangling modifier* or *past perfect participle*? Will he be on the street corner with a sign? Well, perhaps, but not because of a lack of grammar knowledge. What if the unlearned skill is simple arithmetic (addition, subtraction, multiplication, division)? That could be an issue as this type of math is used for everything from following a cookie recipe to figuring out how much a 75% discount on games would come to.

So, if you are worried about a particular skill, take time to imagine what would happen if he or she did not learn it. Many times the answer is *nothing*.

Second, remember that just because your child does not know something *now* does not mean he will not learn it later when he needs it. Percentages may be abstract and dull right now but when she gets that first part-time job waiting tables and is trying to figure out how big a tip she hopes to get, it is important. Spelling is boring until he starts emailing with the cute girl he met at the library and he wants to look smarter. Penmanship (a dying skill!) may be tedious but if she has to sign in on a worksheet each day at her volunteer job, she does not want her signature to look childish.

Learning a skill because you *need* it is traditionally much faster and more enduring than learning it because you are *supposed to*. (Think about books you choose to read versus those your teachers made you read. Quite a difference!) If a skill has a concrete purpose to it rather than just being something someone your age is supposed to know, it gains relevance. The concept that a child of a given age is supposed to learn and know certain material is, once again, a public school model, and one that you *do not need to follow*.

Now you can finish the statement: If my children do not learn how to _____, it is okay because either they will never actually need it or, if they do, they will learn it then.

Feel better?

Further Resources on This Topic

"Homeschooling the Late Bloomer"
http://www.homeschoolnewslink.com/homeschool/articles/
   vol5iss5/thelatebloomer.shtml

"Encouraging Reading in *Late* Readers"
http://www.vahomeschoolers.org/articles/encouraging_late_
   readers.asp

63. *When in the day should I start and when should I stop?*

The key is not to prioritize what's on your schedule, but to schedule your priorities.

—Stephen Covey

If you have been reading these questions in order, you will know the answer: Whenever you want to! Keeping in mind that the typical homeschooling day (the hours directly spent on education, not on field trips, talking, playing, and so on) is rarely more than two to three hours (depending on the age of your child), you have a lot of hours to manipulate however you want.

Think about your child's personality, as well as your own. Are you morning people? Or do you really kick into gear in the afternoon or even evening? Use the answer to those questions to guide you as to when to do your primary teaching. If your child struggles with short attention spans, you can do an hour, take a break, and then do another hour later. Please discard the 8-to-3 public school model, as it simply does not apply to the homeschooling environment.

Work your homeschooling around other elements, such as your or your partner's work schedule, lessons, sport events, practices, and play dates. In other words, customize it to fit your family and its needs. You have 24 hours to work with—make the most of them.

Further Resources on This Topic

Different types of schedules and scheduling tips
http://www.homeschooling-ideas.com/home-school-schedule.html

Unschooling record keeper and schedule form
http://www.thehomeschoolmom.com/gettingorganized/planner
.php#unschool

64. When can I homeschool if I am a single parent or my partner and I both work?

We can get too easily bogged down in the academic part of home-schooling, a relatively minor part of the whole, which is to raise competent, caring, literate, happy people.

—Diane Flynn Keith

Now that you know, from reading other questions in this section, that homeschooling takes less time than you thought and can be done at any time of day (or night) that works best for you, this question is easier to answer.

If both you and your partner work, or if you are a single parent, you can still homeschool but it may take a little more ingenuity and creative, out-of-the box thinking than you might have done. Perhaps you and your partner can work split shifts or swing shifts so that someone is at home (and awake) during the hours you want to homeschool. You could try squeezing all of your homeschooling into weekend hours or whatever free hours you have from work. If you are divorced, you might be able to arrange homeschooling time with your ex (dividing the subjects between you, for example). If your children are older, you can try relying on independent study and/or online courses for the bulk of your homeschooling.

Sit down and brainstorm the question with your partner or ex and your kids. They might have ideas that you had not considered. Remember that whatever you start off with is not written in stone—you can change and tinker with it as you see what works and what does not.

Further Resources on This Topic

The single parent homeschool (SPA)
www.singleparenthomeschool.com

Single homeschooling
http://www.homeeducator.com/FamilyTimes/articles/9-2article 15.htm

65. When are we able to use public school resources?

The home is the first and most effective place to learn the lessons of life: truth, honor, virtue, self control, the value of education, honest work, and the purpose and privilege of life. Nothing can take the place of home in rearing and teaching children, and no other success can compensate for failure in the home.

—David O. McKay

Some homeschoolers want to utilize the resources and materials found in the public school system, and understandably, they turn to their closest school to request it. They do not always get the reaction they had hoped for.

How likely is your school to share with you as you homeschool? Unfortunately, there is no comprehensive answer to this question because it depends completely on the attitude of the public school district where you live. Some are extremely open to homeschoolers and invite them to use any and all of their resources, while others are just the opposite and have a very negative attitude that translates into *Keep out of our school and any of its resources*. Some schools invite homeschoolers to use the playground and library, be part of the school band, orchestra, or choir, take driver education, participate in plays, and so on. Others do not allow any of this.

How do you know which way your school administration feels about the issue? Call and ask the principal's thoughts. Ask whether services can be used and if so, which ones and at what times. Ask whether you need to sign some kind of insurance waiver (you often do) or fill out any other paperwork. If the principal is clearly against doing anything with homeschoolers, you must decide how hard you want to pursue it. Perhaps a bad experience in the past with a homeschooler has made the principal wary. Your children might be the ones to change that impression and repair the damage. Many public school officials labor under the same myths and misunderstandings about homeschooling as the general public. You may find yourself motivated enough to try and correct the confusion. On the other hand, some public school administrations are downright hostile and close-minded about homeschoolers. In that case, you would do well to back out rather than go into battle. There are very, very few resources (if any) that your public school has that you cannot find elsewhere.

Further Resources on This Topic

Making sure all students receive adequate music education
http://www.menc.org/about/view/homeschooled-students
   -participation-in-public-school-music-education\

The ongoing relationships between public school and homeschoolers
http://www.articlesbase.com/homeschooling-articles/
   homeschooling-vs-public-school-can-we-all-get-along
   -1230945.html

66. When (at what age) should I start/stop homeschooling?

What is most important and valuable about the home as a base for children's growth into the world is not that it is a better school than the schools, but that it isn't a school at all.

—John Holt

Surprise! You have been homeschooling from the moment you became a parent. Teaching your child is part of daily parenting. Even if you decide to enroll your child in kindergarten, if she is already able to walk, talk, use the bathroom, tie her shoes, and so on, it is because you taught her during the last five-plus years. You just might not have realized it at the time.

When you start is not really part of the question. But do you shift from just parenting to homeschooling? That is up to you, your partner, and your child (heard that a few times before, haven't you?). Just because public school has targeted five or six years old as the beginning does not mean you have to. Many children are not remotely prepared for official classes or teaching of any kind at that age.

Homeschooling begins at birth—and with any luck continues until the day we die. However, official homeschooling starts whenever you want it to. (Is coloring homeschooling? making food in the kitchen? singing the Alphabet Song? Yes!) How long you go is entirely—yes, once again—up to you. Some parents think they will try it for one month, one grade, one year—and take it from there. Others plan to do it only through elementary school, junior high, or high school. Each family is different and if you polled first-year homeschoolers and asked them, you'd get entirely different answers than what they actually end up doing. Home education is an evolving process, constantly undergoing change. Many who start out to do one month end up homeschooling all the way through high school graduation. Others never make it that far.

Deciding right now—as you are exploring and starting to homeschool—how long to do it is really a mistake. That would be like deciding in the first five minutes of a basketball game what the final score is going to be. You simply do not have enough information. Take it a week, a month, or a year at a time and see where it leads you and your family.

Further Resources on This Topic

Resources and articles about homeschooling older kids
http://homeschooling.gomilpitas.com/olderkids/OlderKids.htm
http://homeschooling.about.com/od/highschool/High_School_
    Resources.htm

How

THIS SECTION OF the book moves beyond the philosophical questions into the practical matters of homeschools. You will quickly notice that, just like the other sections, this one is not going to tell you the *right* way to do anything, because it does not exist. The only right way for your family to homeschool is the one that works for you. You are happy, your kids are happy, and everyone is learning. The ideas in this section are simply that: *ideas*. Take the ones you like and put the others back on the shelf for later on when you are thinking about changing a few things.

Just for Laughs—Top 10 Reasons to Criminalize Homeschooling

In an effort to increase the public drumbeat for criminalizing homeschooling, a memo has been distributed containing the top 10 reasons why public schooling is better than homeschooling. Here is an excerpt from that memo:

1. Most parents were educated in the underfunded public school system, and so are not smart enough to home-school their own children.

2. Children who receive one-on-one homeschooling will learn more than others, giving them an unfair advantage in the marketplace. This is undemocratic.

3. How can children learn to defend themselves unless they have to fight off bullies on a daily basis?

4. Ridicule from other children is important to the socialization process.

5. Children in public schools can get more practice *Just Saying No* to drugs, cigarettes, and alcohol.

6. Fluorescent lighting may have significant health benefits.

7. Publicly asking permission to go to the bathroom teaches young people their place in society.

8. The fashion industry depends upon the peer pressure that only public schools can generate.

9. Public schools foster cultural literacy, passing on important traditions like the singing of *Jingle Bells, Batman smells, Robin laid an egg...*

10. Homeschooled children may not learn important office career skills, like how to sit still for six hours straight.

67. How do I provide my child with transcripts and a diploma?

Education is the period during which you are being instructed by somebody you do not know, about something you do not want to know.

—G.K. Chesterton

If your child is planning on going to college, the question of transcripts and a diploma often comes up as part of the admissions process. (Although some job applications ask about a diploma, typically you just check a *yes/no* box. Since homeschooling is legal, you can create and print out your own diploma and keep it on hand. This way your teen can check *yes* without qualms. Employers virtually never ask to see it, and if they do, it is legal.) You can create your own transcripts for your children as well; just be sure to use the correct terminology and details. Include extracurricular activities and internships, along with vitals such as full legal name, Social Security number, physical address, and the name of your homeschool. If you have kept records, you can rely on them for much of this, and you can also brainstorm with your partner and children. Among all of you, you will be better able to remember what classes and field trips were taken. Go online or find a public school transcript to use as a model or talk to a public school teacher who can provide some guidance.

If you have homeschooled all the way through high school rather than enrolling in any kind of correspondence or distance learning program, your next best option is having your child take the GED (Graduate Equivalent Degree) test. Most colleges will accept this in place of a diploma.

Be aware, however, that transcripts, diplomas and test scores are not mandatory for college admission. As homeschooling as grown, many universities and colleges have also adjusted their admissions requirements. (Universities love homeschoolers!) For example, a rising number of institutions accept portfolios instead of standardized test scores and transcripts.

A portfolio can consist of many different items, depending on your child, your years of homeschooling, and your philosophy. Here are a few common examples:

- journal of activities and progress
- list of resources and curricula used
- samples of writing or drawing
- photographs of field trips, award ceremonies, and projects
- list of books read
- letters of personal and professional reference
- resume

Creating the paperwork you will need for college admissions seems intimidating but if you take it slowly, get advice, and have decent records (or just a good memory!), you can do it.

Further Resources on This Topic

"Transcripts Made Easy: The Homeschooler's Guide to High
   School Paperwork"
http://www.everyday-education.com/tme/index.shtml

How to create different parts of the portfolio
http://www.donnayoung.org/forms/planners/portfolio.htm

The Homeschooler's Guide to Porfolios and Transcripts, by
   Loretta Heuer, MEd
"Transcript Boot Camp on DVD," by Inge Cannon (DVD)

68. How do I homeschool about a subject I do not understand?

An education isn't how much you have committed to memory, or even how much you know. It is being able to differentiate between what you do know and what you do not.

—Anatole France

No single person knows and understands everything about every subject: teachers and parents included. When you homeschool your child, unless you are only working with the first few elementary school grades, you are sure to encounter subjects you do not remember or simply do not know. What then?

You have a number of options:

1. **You can learn the subject along with your child.** Why not just learn this material together as a team? It can be a bonding experience between you and your child and it gives you additional knowledge.

2. **You can ask your partner to teach this subject.** Maybe this is one your partner knows much better. In that case, let it be his or her turn.

3. **You can barter with someone else to teach this subject.** Perhaps you know someone who knows this subject well. Offer to babysit, bake, clean, walk the dog—whatever they need in return for lessons.

4. **You can hire a tutor to teach this subject.** Tutors are available for any subject. Check with local schools and colleges, in the yellow pages, online, and on bulletin boards for ads, plus ask others for recommendations.

5. **You can purchase a curriculum and/or other materials that teach this subject.** If you do not know the topic, you can always buy an entire course that teaches it and let it be the professor for a while.

6. **You can enroll your child in a class that teaches this subject.** Perhaps there is a community college, high school, or noncredit course that your child can take in this subject area. Look into area college catalogs and on websites for what is available.

7. **You can find a volunteer or internship that teaches this subject.** Many children learn best in a hands-on environment. Working on site as a volunteer or by interning is a great way to learn a tough subject.

8. **You can ask another homeschooler or homeschooling parent to teach this subject.** Check with your local support group and see whether there is someone who is willing to teach this subject to your child in return for you teaching your best subject to one of their kids. Older homeschoolers might also be interested in tutoring younger ones.

Clearly, coming up against a topic you do not know well enough to teach yourself is not a large problem because there are so many possible solutions. In many ways, it is actually an opportunity in disguise because it allows you the chance to stretch and reach out a little further. What you find might even surprise you.

Further Resources on This Topic

The Complete Guide to Successful Co-oping for Homeschooling Families, by Linda Koeser and Lori Marse

"Maybe We Would be Amazed"
http://www.maybewewouldbeamazed.com/coops.html

69. How do I homeschool a gifted child?

Essentially, there are as many methods of learning as there are children. William Butler Yeats describes education as ". . . not the filling of a pail, but the lighting of a fire." Most classrooms are designed for filling pails, whereas gifted children in particular need the opportunities to fan the flames of their abilities beyond the strict confines of someone else's agenda.

—Corin Barsily Goodwin, Director of Gifted
Homeschoolers Forum

Homeschooling your gifted children may seem daunting but it may be the best thing you can do for them. Gifted children are often lost in the public school classroom, forced to go at a slower (and so, to them, boring) pace or they are placed in special classes that lend themselves to stigma and labels ("Do not talk to her. She's one of those brainy kids.")

Through homeschooling, parents can give their kids the time and freedom to learn as they want without worrying how it compares to their peers. It also gives them flexibility to pursue what interests them. According to Corin Barsily Goodwin from Gifted Homeschoolers, homeschooling gifted kids has many benefits: in addition to alleviating boredom issues and eliminating comparisons with other students, it allows children to "find themselves, both academically and within their community."

Gifted children commonly require a different teaching method, curriculum, and pace than other children. By experiencing all of this at home instead of in the public school system, your children have a chance to develop their wonderful gifts without fear of being left behind or ostracized.

Further Resources on This Topic

Homeschooling Your Gifted Child, by LearningExpress®

Educating Your Gifted Child, by Vicki Carunana

"Gifted Homeschooling in the U.S."
http://giftedhomeschoolers.org/articles/NAGCMagazineSpring09.pdf

70. How do I know whether my child is learning?

Education has produced a vast population able to read but unable to distinguish what is worth reading.

—G. M. Trevelyan

Without regular tests and report cards, you may wonder how you can tell if your child is actually learning. It may be comforting to realize that children are learning every single moment they are awake. It may not be official school material, but they are learning. They are soaking up what is happening around them, from the way you respond to the person on the phone to how the dog is chasing the squirrels in the backyard to how your partner fixes the clogged sink. They hear what is on the radio and on television. They learn from the games they are playing, the magazines they are reading, and the people they are emailing.

How do you know your kids are actually learning what you are teaching? Watch them. Listen to them. Do they answer your questions? Do they move on to the next chapter or lesson in the book? Do they refer to the material when talking to friends or siblings? When you go over the work they did, do they seem confident or confused? All of these are clues as to whether they have learned the material or not. Sure, you can test them—ask them to write out answers or download a test from the Internet—but there are many other ways to figure it out without the stress of tests and grades.

Should you give out grades? If you live in a state that does not require them, they are relatively unnecessary. There is little point in assigning grades in the homeschool environment—this is not a competition or a race. You just want the children to learn the material and if they have, then they have succeeded.

If you live in a state that requires grades as part of the records, that is another story. You can keep track of them in a notebook (report cards are not necessary.) You will also want to keep track of the grades in nineth through twelfth grade if you will need transcripts for college admissions.

Further Resources on This Topic

Homeschool grades
http://www.squidoo.com/homeschool_grading#module4837058

"How Homeschoolers Keep Track of Grades"
http://homeschooling.suite101.com/article.cfm/how_
    homeschoolers_keep_track_of_grades

71. How much does homeschooling cost?

We're not trying to do School at Home. We're trying to do home-school. These are two entirely different propositions. We're not try-

ing to replicate the time, style or content of the classroom. Rather we're trying to cultivate a lifestyle of learning in which learning takes place from morning until bedtime seven days each week. The formal *portion of each teaching day is just the tip of the iceberg.*
　　　　　—Steve and Jane Lambert, homeschooling parents[1]

It is not possible to give a definitive answer to this one because there is just too much variance in styles and requirements. Homeschooling can cost virtually nothing—or it can cost hundreds of dollars per child. There are many examples.

- If you are a relaxed homeschooler/unschooler and you purchase most of your products and materials at garage sales, thrift stores, and swap meets, and you borrow as much as possible from other homeschoolers and the library, your cost is very, very low. On the other hand, if you are a structured homeschooler and you choose to purchase entire packaged curricula and the corresponding textbooks and supplements, it can be very costly.
- If you ask your parents or grandparents or friends to give you memberships and subscriptions as gifts, your costs will go down. If you buy all of these yourself, they will go up.
- If you already have a lot of books, arts and crafts, games, and other supplies in the house, your cost will be less, but if you do not have any, it can go up.
- If you join a state and/or national group that has an annual fee, your costs go up.
- If you attend local or national homeschooling conferences, your costs go up.
- If you do not already have a computer, you will either need to go somewhere (such as a library) to access one on a regular basis to keep costs down, or buy one for your house.

---

[1]http://www.fiveinarow.com

- If you swap with other homeschoolers, your cost goes down.
- If you make your own materials, your cost goes down.
- If you research ways to borrow materials instead of buying them, your costs go down.

As you can see, there is no set cost to homeschooling. You choose what to buy and what not buy. The overall expense should never be a deciding factor in whether or not you choose to homeschool, because you are in control.

Further Resources on This Topic

Budgeting and homeschooling
http://budgethomeschool.com/

72. How can my child return to or enter public school?

To confuse compulsory schooling with equal educational opportunity is like confusing organized religion with spirituality. One does not necessarily lead to the other. Schooling confuses teaching with learning, grade advancement with education, a diploma with competence, and fluency with the ability to say something new.
—Wendy Priesnitz

Homeschooling can last from kindergarten through high school graduation; in some families, that is just what happens. In other families, however, homeschooling may end after a short time or at some determined spot (entering high school is a common point). What happens when you, your partner, your child, or—best of all—all of you decide that it is time to go back to public school?

Assuming reentry is being done for good reasons, the first step is to contact your local school district and ask their process is. Some schools are quite informal and have few requirements. These will admit the child into a set grade based on age. Other schools, may insist on testing to make sure your child is up to grade level in all subjects (more often than not, they are ahead). Some schools may require transcripts.

Once you have done the paperwork required for your children's reentry, make sure they are emotionally prepared to start or return to school. If they have never been to school before, the transition can be quite startling, so it is best to prepare them for the experience. Visit the school beforehand and walk through it (with the administration's permission, of course) so your child can get familiar with where everything is located.

Before your children go back to school, make an agreement as to how long they must stay. Going back to school can be quite involved; make sure they are willing to try it for more than a day or so. On the other hand, an entire year is far too long. A week or two is usually about right. By then, your child will know whether school is what they were hoping for—or not. Reality does not always match what they had imagined from television and movies or from listening to their peers. Either way, be as supportive as possible. This is not an easy decision for anyone.

Further Resources on This Topic

The transition from homeschool to public school
http://homeschooling.suite101.com/article.cfm/from_homeschool_
   to_public_school
http://homeschooling.gomilpitas.com/olderkids/BackNow.htm

73. How can my child be accepted into college?

How do children learn two very difficult skills, walking and talking, without anyone's making a self-conscious effort to teach them? Could children learn other things, even "school" subjects like reading and math, in the same way, by imitating other people's behavior, making mistakes, correcting them on their own, and asking for help when they need it?

—Larry and Susan Kaseman, *Taking Charge
through Homeschooling*

With every passing year, it gets easier for homeschoolers to get accepted in the colleges of their choice. Where once they were looked on as oddities and scrutinized by puzzled college admissions officers, today they are not only commonplace but desired by many institutions. Recent surveys have demonstrated the following:

- College professors rank homeschoolers in the top tier academically.
- Nearly 80% of homeschooled children test above the national average and 54.7% in the top quarter.
- 44% of colleges already have verbal or written policies for homeschool applicants.
- 96% of colleges polled had at least one and sometimes more than 200 homeschooled students enrolled.

Homeschoolers do not always have the transcripts and national test scores that the average college applicant has, but that is becoming less and less of a problem as time goes by. Instead, colleges are opening their policies to include portfolios and other alternative record keeping.

If your children are interested in attending college, contact the schools they prefer to see what their policies are. If you are looking far into the future—for example, for your homeschooled first grader—the policies will have changed dramatically. By that time, homeschooling will most likely be a minor concern, if not irrelevant.

Further Resources on This Topic

Homeschool-friendly colleges and universities
http://www.homeschoolfriendlycolleges.com/
http://learninfreedom.org/colleges_4_hmsc.html

College admission requirements for homeschoolers
Cafi Cohen, *Homeschoolers' College Admissions Handbook: Preparing Your 12-to-18-Year-Old for a Smooth Transition*

74. How do I decide what kind of curriculum to use?

All I am saying . . . can be summed up in two words: Trust Children.
Nothing could be more simple, or more difficult. Difficult because to
trust children we must first learn to trust ourselves, and most of us
were taught as children that we could not be trusted.

—John Holt

There has been a great deal of discussion about homeschooling
philosophies and styles throughout this book. There have also been
answers about curriculum choices. Before you can decide on any
type of curriculum, you must ask yourself (and fully answer) these
questions:

- Am I leaning more towards structured homeschooling or
  unschooling?
- What materials do I already have on hand?
- What is my child's learning style?
- How formally do I want to teach my child?
- How much money do I have to spend?
- How many materials can I borrow instead of purchasing?
- What types of materials does my child tend to prefer?
- At what grade level is my child in all of the major subjects?
- How much research have I done on what types of curricula are
  available?
- Do I want a religious- or a secular-based curriculum?

Once you have these answers in place, buying curricula is much easier. You will know whether you need to go online, to a store, the library,
or bargain hunting—or a combination of all these. In the end, the only
people who should decide what kind of curriculum you get are you,
your partner, and your child. Be prepared to make mistakes: You will
almost certainly purchase some things that do no more than gather
dust on the shelf (just think of some of your exercise equipment in the
garage!). Someone will not like a particular item—your child will find

it boring, or you will find it confusing or poorly done, or vice versa. It is all part of the process but if you plan for it, you will not feel nearly as bad.

Further Resources on This Topic

Reviews (by parents and organizations) of some of the
   homeschooling products on the market
http://homeschooling.about.com/od/productreviews/Product_
   Reviews_Homeschooling_Products.htm

Resource guide to curricula
http://www.homeschool.com/

75. How can my child take driver education or go to the prom?

We are shut up in schools and college recitation rooms for ten or fifteen years, and come out at last with a bellyful of words and do not know a thing.

—Ralph Waldo Emerson

As you have learned throughout this book, virtually any opportunity that the public school has to offer can be duplicated or even surpassed within homeschooling if you know where to look. This also holds true for two of the events traditionally associated with public school: driver education and the prom.

How do homeschooling teens learn how to drive? If they cannot take the school course, getting their license can be a difficult experience. Here are some ideas.

- A number of companies offer online driver education courses, practice tests, and traffic school. A simple online search can yield many different possibilities.
- You can order used driver ed textbooks from online companies such as Amazon or find them in thrift stores in the textbook or education book section.

- Stop by your local driver's license branch and pick up a free manual for your state's driving rules so your child can study it at home.
- For practice, your child can take sample tests online.
- Check with your local school district to see whether your homeschooler can enroll in their driver education courses. Be aware, however, that some public schoolers are not always friendly to homeschoolers; you do not want to put your teen into an awkward social situation.
- Wait until your teen is 18 and teach him or her yourself and then go and get a learner's permit.

As for the prom: Many teens do not care a whit about the prom and cannot fathom why people might be upset at the idea of not having one. Others want the opportunity to dress up, get flowers, and dance! Homeschooling support groups all over the country have organized and held their own proms for years. In Oregon, for example, a home-school prom has been held for six years in a row and each time, it draws more than 100 teens from the area. The prom takes place in a downtown ballroom, and features refreshments, photos, a live DJ, and even prom king and queen. Also in Oregon, the Not Back to School Camp, an annual camp for homeschooling teens, includes a prom as part of its activities.

Further Resources on This Topic

State-by-state listings on how homeschoolers can get their driver's license
http://homeschooling.gomilpitas.com/explore/driversedstate.htm

How to host your own prom, from decorations to locations
http://home-school.lovetoknow.com/Homeschool_Prom

List of upcoming homeschooling proms
http://homeschooling.gomilpitas.com/articles/102303.htm

76. How do I deal with rude relatives, nosy neighbors, and crabby coworkers?

It is a miracle that curiosity survives formal education.

—Albert Einstein

The quick and simple answer: Ignore them. Would you care what they had to say about the church you go to, the food you eat, the way you style your hair, or what books you read? Why let their opinions about your educational preferences bother you?

This may sound glib but it is true. If the people who have negative things to say about your decision to homeschool are not relevant to your life, let their comments roll off your back. If they are open to learning about homeschooling, you can decide whether you want to take the time to educate them—or not.

However, sometimes the negative people are ones whose opinions are important to you, especially relatives or friends. In that case, you deal with their behavior in the same way you would if they had something negative or intrusive to say about your other lifestyle choices. You ignore a certain element and then you find the most effective and polite way to respond. Often a simple discussion is enough to fix the problem or at least alleviate the unpleasantness. At some point, if you have tried patience and education, you may find that the best solution is to avoid the entire topic—or, in worst case scenarios, avoid the person as well. No one knows what is better for your child than you and your partner. Other opinions may have validity, but in the end, this is your decision alone.

Further Resources on This Topic

Advice on handling homeschool critics

http://www.ehow.com/how_2132327_deal-homeschool-criticism
.html

http://hubpages.com/hub/Homeschooling-Unsuportive-Family
-Members

77. How does my child get a job?

Schooling, instead of encouraging the asking of questions, too often discourages it.

—Madeleine L' Engle

Getting a job is often easier for homeschooled teens than it is for public-schooled teens. They are more employable because they tend to have far more available hours each day to work. Finding a job is the same for a homeschooling teen as it is for any teen—reading the ads, asking around, checking bulletin boards—the usual routine. References are often easy to obtain for homeschoolers as they tend to have many different contacts within the community.

Homeschooling teens often find jobs within the homeschooling community itself. They work for other families, babysitting, doing paperwork or yard work, cleaning, walking dogs, and so on. Often asking around within your support group is an effective way to find at least temporary part-time jobs.

Of course, teen work permits are still required, homeschooling or not. Most states require them for kids under the age of 14 except for those working on farms, gardens, or orchards, as volunteers, in a family-owned business, occasional work around someone's home, or work for state or local government. Each state has slightly different requirements, so be sure to check with yours.

Further Resources on This Topic

Details about work permits for your teen
http://www.internjobs.com/jobSeekers/resources/articles/Teen_
    Permits_14-15.html

What teens need to do before getting a job
http://www.associatedcontent.com/article/1113134/teens_and_
    work_permits_do_i_need_a.html?cat=17

78. How do my children learn how to deal with conflict if they do not go to school?

The aim of public education is not to spread enlightenment at all; it is simply to reduce as many individuals as possible to the same safe level, to breed a standard citizenry, to put down dissent and originality.
—H.L. Mencken

It says a lot about public school that many people wonder how children will learn how to cope with conflict and unhappiness if they do not spend their youth sitting in a classroom. However, many homeschoolers ask: If children do not go to school, how will they develop the ability to deal with trouble and misery? How will they know how to handle bullies or overly demanding authorities? How will they be able to cope with peer competition and pressure?

Sadly enough, the answer is: The world will teach them. Whether or not children are in school, they will certainly have more than enough opportunity to encounter unpleasant people and situations that they will have to learn how to deal with, one way or another. They will have to learn how to compete, whether it is with a sibling over who gets to play the new Playstation® game first or with a peer who is up for the same part-time job. They will learn how to deal with rude and obnoxious people on the street, at work, in a store, or anywhere else. They will feel peer pressure the first time they go to a party where everyone is smoking, drinking, or doing anything else dangerous.

It is an unfortunate fact that the world is full of opportunities for kids to learn how to deal with trouble—public school is only one of countless avenues. At least, through homeschooling, parents can give their children a few extra years of protection and a chance to mature a bit more before they come face to face and must deal with life's inevitable conflicts.

Further Resources on This Topic

"Why We Fight: How Public Schools Cause Social Conflict"
http://www.cato.org/pub_display.php?pub_id=7040

School and bullies
http://www.psparents.net/Bullying.htm

79. How do I homeschool kids of different ages or grade levels?

The geniuses of the ages were generally brought up in home schools.
                                                        —Raymond Moore

The shortest answer is: With a great deal of creativity and patience.

The longer, more helpful answer is: You can do it but you may have to practice your juggling skills a little bit more. It is certainly possible to homeschool children of different ages. How challenging it is depends greatly on the age of your children. If they are more than 10 or 12 years old and less than three or four years apart, for example, you can merge their lessons fairly easily. They can often learn the same thing at the same time (if your mind balks at that, it probably means that you are still stuck in that public-school model of thinking!). Unit studies are especially good for working with multiple ages as these can easily be adapted to different skill levels.

If your children are young, multiple ages can be a little more difficult. You can work with the youngest one first and then put her to coloring, looking through books, or napping while you work with the older ones. Or you can work with the oldest first and then give him some independent work to focus on while you are with the younger ones.

You can call reinforcements in to help you as well. While you homeschool one child, an older child, grandparent, partner, or friend can be spending time with the others.

If you find yourself getting stressed out from trying to juggle too much at one time, take a break. Throw out the schedule and go on a field trip. Bake cookies. Go outside and feed the squirrels. Find something else to do until you are all relaxed and having fun again. Tomorrow is another day.

Further Resources on This Topic

Tips for homeschooling multiple age and skill levels
http://math-and-reading-help-for-kids.org/articles/Tips_for_
   homeschooling_multiple_age_and_skill_levels.html

How to homeschool multiple children
http://www.ehow.com/how_5609586_homeschool-multiple
   -children.html

80. How do my child and I stay motivated?

Learning can only happen when a child is interested. If he's not interested it is like throwing marshmallows at his head and calling it eating.

—Anonymous

You have been homeschooling for weeks—even months. Everything is going along just fine until suddenly you, your partner, or your child hits a wall. Motivation is gone. What happened?

First of all, do not be surprised when this happens. It happens to people in all aspects of life—with a job, with a hobby, with a relationship. All these are exciting at first but then lose their allure as the newness wears off. This sudden lack of motivation certainly happens all the time in public school.

The key to getting past this inevitable roadblock is to see if you can figure out what is causing the problem and then change it. For example, maybe you have lost motivation because you feel as though too much responsibility is resting on your shoulders. In this case, it is time to delegate and let others relieve you some of the burden. Or perhaps your son or daughter is struggling because the style of teaching being used does not fit his or her personality and pace. If so, it is time to try something new. Get different material. Find a different way to teach it. Try another topic. Perhaps you have been focusing hard on a set topic and enthusiasm has run out. It may be time for a field trip, or to take a day or two off and read or go to the movies.

By varying activities as much as possible and by making sure that everyone involved has the freedom to say *I'm tired of this* or *This isn't working* or *I'm bored*, you will find you have less trouble maintaining motivation and will be better able to avoid burnout (see Question 88).

Further Resources on This Topic

How to motivate your child

http://www.eclectichomeschool.org/articles/article.asp?articleid=292

http://www.helium.com/knowledge/164808-motivating-your
  -homeschooled-child

81. How does my child graduate?

To control and sort young people for the sake of institutional efficiency is to crush the human spirit.

—Ron Miller

How do you know when it is time to graduate from home school? Once again, the answer is: It is up to you or to the independent study or distance learning program or umbrella school your children are using. You might decide your children are done when they pass their GED or when they are given a diploma by their school. Other families decide the time to graduate is based on the age of the homeschooler, time spent on courses, acceptance into college, or the young person's evaluation of his or her own readiness to move on to the next level.

How can you decide? What homeschooling program you are using may be a deciding factor. It may have certain criteria that must be matched before a diploma is issued. Have your child take the GED and see how he or she does. Talk to your teen and see how he or she feels about being done with high school. As author Cafi Cohen writes, "Consider your experience with education and the relationship of formal and informal education to life. And then—here's the hard part—trust yourself. Do what makes the most sense for your situation."[2]

---

[2]http://www.homeedmag.com/HEM/HEM154.98/154.98_clmn_ok.html

Once the decision has been made, consider a backyard party or some other kind of official celebration. Graduation is an important event that should be noted (plus your teen can get those great graduation presents!).

Further Resources on This Topic

Ideas for planning a graduation party or celebration
http://homeschool-graduation.suite101.com/article.cfm/planning_a_
    homeschool_graduation

Templates for creating diplomas (including gold lettering)
http://homeschooling.gomilpitas.com/articles/060303.htm

82. How do I create a unit study?

I am entirely certain that twenty years from now we will look back at education as it is practiced in most schools today and wonder that we could have tolerated anything so primitive.

—John W. Gardner

Unit studies are wonderful tools because they can be tailored to fit every style, from structured homeschooling to unschooling. A unit study is simply a set of educational activities that centers around a set idea, topic, or interest. You can create your own from a mix of materials or you can purchase packaged unit studies from many companies.

For example, let us say that your child is fascinated by airplanes. If you wanted to create a unit study based on this passion, you might do any or all of the following activities (depending on the age of your child):

- visit an aviation museum
- visit the home of a famous pilot
- read biographies of the Wright Brothers, Amelia Earhart, the Tuskegee Airmen, and so on

- make paper airplanes
- tour a large and a small airport
- meet and talk with pilots, air traffic controllers, aviation service technicians, and other staff
- study aircraft engines
- study the principles of aerodynamics
- purchase and play with remote-controlled planes
- build plastic models of airplanes
- draw plane schematics
- watch films about airplanes (fictional and documentaries)
- get an internship at a local airport
- get pilot lessons
- surf the Web for information about planes, aviation, and related topics
- go to a teacher's supply store for workbooks
- become a member of the EEA Young Eagles program (http://www.youngeagles.org/)
- attend an air show
- play computer and video games based on flight
- explore the Coast Guard and arrange for a tour

Unit studies can be adapted to any age, learning style, and interest. They can be quite fun and can create a lifelong fascination for a topic or even spark a future career. They are one of the best parts of homeschooling and make learning fun!

Further Resources on This Topic

Alphabetical list of unit study topics and ideas
http://www.thehomeschoolmom.com/schoolroom/unitstudies.php

Unit study directory
http://homeschooling.about.com/cs/unitstudies/a/unitdirectory.htm

83. How does the computer figure in homeschooling?

If a child cannot learn the way we teach, maybe we should teach the way they learn.

—Ignacio Estrada

Over the last decade, the personal home computer has become an integral part of most households. Do you absolutely need one in order to homeschool? Certainly not. Generations of homeschoolers have done great without one. Does having one make it easier? Definitely.

Computers help in a number of ways. They make writing reports, essays, and research papers far easier and faster. Keyboarding often helps students with spelling and grammar skills.

Home computers unequivocally improve the research process because they make it possible to access unlimited, up-to-date information and materials. Computers allow your child to get involved in online forums (a blessing and a curse depending on which ones they go to), that can connect them to other homeschoolers throughout the country. Computers also guide your sons and daughters to online courses and colleges so they can utilize distance-learning programs.

In recent years, the computer has also been an important conduit for social networking. Between Facebook®, MySpace®, Twitter®, and other networks, young people stay in touch online. They IM (instant message) and send emails constantly. While they can do all of this without a computer at home, having one certainly makes homeschooling easier—and often far more fun.

Further Resources on This Topic

Companies that give homeschoolers discounts on software and hardware
http://homeschooling.gomilpitas.com/directory/ComputerShop.htm

Online homeschooling curricula
http://www.homeschool.com/onlinecourses/

84. How do I deal with the issue of truancy?

You cannot teach anybody anything. You can only help them discover it within themselves.

—Galileo

Your child will not be declared truant if you have informed the public school system that you are homeschooling. However, if your son or daughter is out without you during the school day, they may be stopped. As more cities across the country have created Daytime Curfew Laws, this has become a growing problem. These laws basically make it illegal for a child under the age of 18 to be in a public place during set school hours.

To forestall potential problems, many parents are choosing to create homeschool identification cards. These cards typically state the child's name and address and specify that he or she is a homeschooler. If a law enforcement or truancy officer stops your child, this card can help prove that truancy is not a problem.

Identification cards can be made on a home computer but may look handmade and therefore may not always carry the authenticity that some officers prefer. A number of companies that provide products to homeschoolers have begun offering identification cards, as well as similar items such as field trip badges. These items are fairly inexpensive and can provide you and your children some priceless peace of mind.

Further Resources on This Topic

ID cards and others resources
http://www.homeschoolid.com/
http://www.homeschooldigitalid.com/

85. How do we best use our library when homeschooling?

Never doubt that a small group of thoughtful committed citizens can change the world: indeed, it is the only thing that ever has.

—Margaret Mead

There are few resources in your city that can help you with homeschooling more than your public library. It is an amazing treasure trove of resources for any homeschooling family. It is little wonder that, in a National Center for Education Statistics survey, 78% of the homeschoolers polled listed their libraries as their primary source of books and curriculum.

Of course, your public library has most of the books you would ever want to check out for yourself and your children, but that is not all. It also offers videos, music, magazines, newspapers, and books on tape (and all for free!). If there is something you want that the library does not have, you can often request the materials to be sent to you through their interlibrary loan program (also for free!).

Along with these resources, libraries also offer reference books, pamphlets, and other noncirculating materials that you can use right there. In addition, they offer classes and workshops, many of them geared specifically to homeschoolers. Libraries also frequently host support groups and other family activities. It is a great spot to hold homeschooling discussions, game days, and other events (all still for free!).

If you do not have a library card, get one. If you live within the city limits, there is no charge for it. If not, there may be a fee; ask for a membership as your next birthday or holiday gift. Be sure to apply for the educator's card—it is the same one teachers receive and it allows you to check out materials for longer periods of time.

Further Resources on This Topic

Libraries and homeschoolers
http://www.schoollibraryjournal.com/article/CA6582320.html

"Loving the Library" (a column published in *Home Education Magazine*)
http://www.homeedmag.com/HEM/223/goodstuff.html

86. How do I prepare my homeschooled kids to take a standardized test?

No use to shout at them to pay attention. If the situations, the materials, the problems before the child do not interest him, his attention

*will slip off to what does interest him, and no amount of exhortation
or threats will bring it back.*

—John Holt

If you live in a state that requires regular testing at certain grade levels, you need to prepare your child to take these tests. To view practice tests for the SAT, ACT, and other major national tests, you can go to your local bookstore and buy test prep books published by major test prep companies such as LearningExpress®, or you can visit an online test prep site such as www.learnatest.com. Getting familiar with test formats will help ease a great deal of test anxiety. Practice tests give your child an idea of what the tests are like and what the questions will cover. They will also allow you to find out ahead of time what areas are weakest with your child and give you the chance to work on those subjects before it is time to take the test.

Start by doing the tests together and then have your children go through a few tests alone. Finally, add the timed element so they learn to work thoroughly but quickly.

Be sure to talk to your child about these tests and point out that they are not a major issue—nothing worth stressing over, at least. Sure, they should be taken seriously, but a bad score is not the end of the world either. These tests are just a benchmark guide (and not even a terribly reliable one) that can help you figure out strengths and weaknesses. Make taking the test fun—and go out for ice cream or a movie afterwards to celebrate it being done for another few years.

Further Resources on This Topic

SAT and ACT prep titles by LearningExpress®:

411 SAT Critical Reading Questions

411 SAT Algebra & Geometry Questions

411 SAT Writing Questions Essay Prompts

SAT Math Essentials

SAT Writing Essentials

ACT Essay Practice

ACT Preparation in a Flash

87. How do I remove my child from school?

Any child who can spend an hour or two a day, or more if he wants, with adults that he likes, who are interested in the world and like to talk about it, will on most days learn far more from their talk than he would learn in a week of school.

—John Holt

This is an easy one. You write a letter of intent to your school district, with copies for your child's superintendent or principal and one to keep. (Check your state laws and regulations to see if anything additional is required—it rarely, if ever, is.) Dozens of examples of such letters can be found on the Internet but they are all basically the same:

Date

Principal
Name of School
Street Address
City, State, and Zip

Re: Notice of Intent to Homeschool

Dear Principal _____ ,

We are hereby notifying you of our intent to homeschool our son/daughter _____ for the rest of this school year. For your records, the student is:

Your Child's Name _____
Your Street Address _____
Your City, State, and Zip _____
Your Child's Date of Birth _____
Grade: _____

Sincerely,

[Your Name and signature]

It is important to keep your letter simple and not give any more information than necessary. If you want to make sure that the letters are correctly delivered, send them by certified mail with return receipt.

Further Resources on This Topic

Sample letter of intent to homeschool
http://www.americanhomeschools.com/Resources/fill-in_forms/
   Letter_Of_Intent.htm

Sample letter of withdrawal in order to homeschool
http://www.americanhomeschools.com/Resources/fill-in_forms/
   Letter_Of_Withdrawal.htm

88. How do my kids and I avoid getting burned out?

If you are feeling stressed, you are doing too much. Cut back. Lighten up. Time is on your side.
                              —Micki Colfax, *Homeschooling for Excellence*

Just as with losing motivation, burnout is not uncommon in homeschooling—or at work, in class, in relationships, with hobbies. Almost anything you spend a lot of time doing is at risk of burnout. Symptoms include crying easily, losing patience, overreacting to things, making bad decisions, yelling at your spouse or your kids, feeling resentful, angry, and overwhelmed.

There are a number of reasons for reaching this point and all of them can be addressed without throwing in the towel and going back to the public school option. Here are some of the most common reasons families burn out:

1. **You are trying to do too much at one time.** You cannot be everything to everyone all the time without eventual emotional and physical collapse. So often homeschoolers try to fit everything in: field trips, classes, work, chores, errands, lessons, play dates, and more. If you are racing to get it all done and still get a

night of sleep, something needs to go. Reduce any unnecessary outside activities or responsibilities. Every homeschool curriculum needs rest time built in—time to nap, read, relax, pursue hobbies—anything that is soothing and fun. If you do not make room for it, someone is headed for a meltdown.

2. **You want everything to be *perfect* or you have unrealistic expectations.** It is easy to put too much pressure on yourself to make sure everything in your life is flawless. The house is always clean. The kids are clearly prodigies. Your hair and clothing are perfect. You lost ten pounds, your cholesterol is down, and your nails have never looked better. Sure, this is an exaggeration but it is based on truth. You may have completely unrealistic expectations and when you cannot meet them (because you are human!), you begin to unravel. Lighten up! Perfection is not possible, so quit aiming for it. Your children will bicker, the house will get messy, you will get tired, and dinner will be burnt. That's life, and accepting it will help make mistakes and problems much easier to take.

3. **You are using the wrong curriculum.** This has been discussed earlier but bears repeating. If you, your partner, or your child is burning out on homeschooling, take a close look at the curriculum you are using. Is the grade level too high (confusing) or too low (boring)? Is it emphasizing the wrong kind of learning style for your child? Is it too limiting or too abstract? Is it on topics that your child cannot relate to? Try something new. Borrow it. Check it out from the library. Pick it up at a garage sale. Flexibility is an integral part of homeschooling.

4. **You are using the wrong homeschooling methods.** This has also been discussed at length in different parts of the book but is also worth going over again. Burnout often stems from using the wrong method of homeschooling for your family. Perhaps it is too structured, putting too large a burden on everyone involved. Or perhaps it is too loose and vague and no one is sure what they are supposed to be doing. Again, the best advice is: Try something new. Whatever end of the spec-

trum you are leaning toward, go in the opposite direction. See what happens.

5. **You are not getting the support and encouragement you need.** Homeschooling can be lonely if you do not have the support you need. The most important support of all, of course, is that of your partner and your children. After that, it is helpful to have the support of family and friends, although that may take some time to achieve. The encouragement and guidance of a support group are also very useful and can help ease tension and burnout through sharing and empathizing. If you are feeling a lack of the support you need to cope with the demands of homeschooling, reach out and ask for it.

6. **You are dealing with another life-changing event, such as a new job, a new baby, or a new location.** Having a baby, getting a new job, or moving are amazingly stressful events (albeit usually happy ones) and when combined with other life demands, including homeschooling, it is not surprising if burnout results. During any life transition, consider putting homeschooling on pause. Just wait a while until your family has had the chance to acclimate to the changes and then get back to it. Remember that homeschooling breaks are yours to choose and use.

Burnout means that something is wrong—but the decision to home-school is not that reason. Explore the source of your feelings and see what you can do about them. Still not sure? Ask other homeschoolers; chances are very strong that they have been there, done that, and have the t-shirt they can lend you.

Further Resources on This Topic

Personal stories about homeschool burnout
http://homeschooling.about.com/od/burnout/Dealing_With_
   Homeschool_Burnout.htm

Home School Burnout: What It is, What Causes It, How to Overcome It, by Raymond and Dorothy Moore

89. How do I learn to write and talk educationalese, and why will I need it?

Our school education ignores, in a thousand ways, the rules of healthy development.

—Emily Blackwell

The term *educationalese* refers to the jargon used in the educational world. As you know from other parts of life, knowing the jargon makes it easier to connect with others when discussing the same subject. If you are going to be interacting with teachers, school districts, superintendents, and even the Department of Education (which you will certainly be doing if you live in a state that requires contact between the two of you or you withdraw your child from school), you should be familiar with their jargon and be able to use them with ease.

You may find yourself in a position of having to translate your style of homeschooling into educationalese in order for it to present the way educators expect. For example, you could call playing soccer twice a week with the support group *routine physical education* and an oral spelling test as you make cookies *English assessment*.

Here are some of the most commonly used terms that you should understand and know how to use.

Assessment: a way of determining whether a child is learning the material being taught; usually in the form of tests or quizzes, oral or written (asking questions about the book she is reading while you are driving to swimming lessons)

Benchmark: a statement that describes what a child is supposed to know at a specific age or grade level (she is in kindergarten and knows the alphabet)

Benchmark performance: how well your child does the above (can she say it backwards too?)

Collaborative/cooperative: learning that is done in small groups (anything he does with a friend, relative, neighbor, or sibling)

Curriculum/curricula: the materials you use to teach your kids (books, workbooks, movies, field trips, internet sites, conversations, television . . . you get the idea)

Distance learning: learning that takes place with the teacher and the student in different locations (your child and his grandparent discussing life during World War II over the phone or through email, it qualifies)

Higher-order questions: questions that require thinking and reflection, rather than a simple answer (*Do you remember why you felt it was all right to lock your brother into the bathroom?*)

Manipulatives: physical objects that are used to represent or model a mathematical concept (pieces of pizza or pie can teach fractions beautifully)

NCLB: No Child Left Behind, an educational act passed by the Bush administration and often used as the foundation for how students are taught and tested in the classroom (at home, it more likely means counting your children before you leave the grocery store to make sure you have all of them)

Rubric: specific criteria or guidelines used to evaluate student work (often these are complicated process steps in school; at home they are more likely to be: *Did you follow the instructions? Did it turn out the way it was supposed to? Did it taste good or work properly or add up correctly? You pass!*)

Further Resources on This Topic

Educational jargon generator
http://www.sciencegeek.net/lingo.html

Detailed glossary of educational terms
http://www.schoolwisepress.com/smart/dict/dict.html

90. How do I homeschool if I am not religious?

Who besides a degraded rabble would voluntarily present itself to be graded and classified like meat? No wonder school is compulsory.
—John Taylor Gatto

If you remember from early in the book when the myths of home-schooling were discussed, one of them was that only religious people homeschool. Where once that idea held a nugget of truth, it no longer does. Today, people of all faiths, as well as agnostics and atheists, home-school. Because of this trend, a rising number of publishers and com-panies are producing textbooks, curriculum, and other materials that have no religious content at all.

Further Resources on This Topic

A nonreligious homeschooling online magazine
www.secular-homeschooling.com

National websites for secular homeschoolers
www.secularhomeschool.com
www.secularhomeschoolers.net

91. How do I handle discipline for improper school behavior?

I suppose it is because nearly all children go to school nowadays, and have things arranged for them, that they seem so forlornly unable to produce their own ideas.

—Agatha Christie

Everyone who has gone to public school knows that being disciplined for what is called *bad* behavior is just part of the school years. Whether you were told to stand in the corner, paddled, sent to the principal's office, or punished in some other way, most likely you do not remem-ber the experience very happily.

So what happens when you homeschool? What do you do to disci-pline a child who misbehaves? This is a tricky question because the concept of *misbehaving* is such an ambiguous one. What qualifies for one family is apt not to make the cut at all with another one. The rules are also far different in the homeschool environment rather than in public school. For example, not raising your hand, talking out of turn, going to the bathroom without permission, and whispering to other students might be punishable at school but certainly not at home. Many times parents discover that the discipline issues their children may have had at school in the past, or the issues they had most worried about, never come up in the homeschool setting.

Before disciplining your child, it is essential that you outline the rules of your homeschool. What is acceptable and what is not? What is appropriate and what is inappropriate behavior? If rules are broken, what is the punishment? All of this should be discussed before you begin so that your child is completely clear on what is acceptable.

What type of discipline you will use, of course, is up to you and should be consistent with whatever type you use for nonhomeschooling infractions. It should be respectful of the child and result in improved behavior, rather than fear or other negative responses. Making sure it is age appropriate is essential as well; a 15-year-old can understand the consequences of his actions far better than a 5-year-old can!

Lastly, it helps to look for the underlying reason behind the misbehavior. Is your child tired? hungry? bored? frustrated? If so, taking care of that problem is going to be more effective than punishing the child for acting out.

The concept of punishing a child for bad behavior is often a part of the public school model, and is not one that parents need to mimic at home. Certainly, children need to learn not to behave inappropriately, rudely, or unkindly but those lessons are more effectively taught through role modeling and loving guidance than through punishment. Home is the perfect place to do so!

Further Resources on This Topic

A reference for handling misbehavior at home and in school
http://www.disciplinehelp.com/parent/

Homeschooling and discipline
http://www.hslda.org/docs/news/washingtontimes/200406210.asp

92. How do I fill in the hours of the day?

There are only two places in the world where time takes precedence over the job to be done. School and prison.

—William Glasser

Most of the time, new homeschoolers ask just the opposite: How in the world am I going to fit everything I need to do into 24 hours? Some, however, are worried that having children home all day, especially if they are used to being in school, will be awkward. How will the time be filled up?

How many hours are actually spent in homeschooling depends, as you have found out many times throughout this book, on a number of factors including the age of your child, how many children you have, and what homeschooling method you follow. Regardless of these factors, though, you are not going to be homeschooling your children for nearly as many hours as they would usually spend in the public school classroom (typically seven to eight hours, including travel time).

So, what will you do all day? Here are some of the most common ways those hours are filled up:

- going on field trips
- running errands
- playing games or cards
- reading books
- studying materials
- doing homework
- attending lessons or workshops
- going to the library
- writing letters
- watching a movie
- going online
- making food—and eating it
- talking to siblings and parents
- walking the dog

- writing papers, journals, and so on
- listening to music
- doing household chores
- cleaning rooms
- taking a walk
- playing sports
- talking to friends by IM, phone, or in person
- drawing pictures

With all of these choices, filling up the hours of the day is rarely difficult. And believe it or not, every single one of these activities is actually a learning experience—just do not tell your kids!

Further Resources on This Topic

Ideas for experiments, worksheets, unit studies, and much more
www.homeschoolfun.com

The Ultimate Book of Homeschooling Ideas: 500+ Fun and Creative Learning Activities for Kids Ages 3–12, by Linda Dobson

93. How do I deal with a partner who is not supportive or helpful?

The millions of dollars which we devote every year to high-school education are, for the most part, money spent for the retarding of intelligence, the discouragement of efficiency, the stunting of character.

—Bernard Iddings Bell

Is it possible to homeschool if your partner is not sold on the idea? Yes. Is it harder? Very much so. You need this person to support and encourage you. You need his or her involvement and assistance. Without it, everything is on your shoulders and that is exhausting even to think about let alone actually do.

The two people who need to be on your side in this family decision are your partner and your child. Together, the three (plus) of you are an invincible team. Remove any one of you and the project becomes much more challenging.

If your partner is not behind you on the idea of homeschooling, talk about it until you understand why. Often it is not a generic I-do-not-like-home-schooling attitude, but a particular element that bothers him or her. If you can pinpoint what it is, then you can work to solve it. Some valid concerns might be that your child will not make friends, learn to read, go to college, or get a job.

Always keep in mind that the reason your partner is so worried is because he or she loves your children and wants the best possible life for them. Knowing that this is the primary motivation behind the objections can soften them a bit.

Talk to your partner about the concern. Have him or her read the pertinent questions and answers in books such as this one. Have him or her surf the web and do some reading. Best of all, have him or her attend a support group meeting where homeschoolers can be seen in real life rather than in the imagination. Watching how normal they are, and seeing how well their children are growing up, can alleviate many concerns. If there is a homeschooling conference in your area, go together. If there is a presentation at the library or a speaker at the church, go together. The more involved your partner is in the learning process about homeschooling, the more he or she is likely to support it and you.

Further Resources on This Topic

The *anti-homeschooling* spouse issue
http://www.successful-homeschooling.com/anti-homeschooling.html

Homeschooling dads and attitudes
http://www.articlesbase.com/homeschooling-articles/
    homeschooling-dads-1320631.html

94. How do I homeschool a child with learning disabilities?

The plain fact is that education is itself a form of propaganda—a deliberate scheme to outfit the pupil, not with the capacity to weigh ideas, but with a simple appetite for gulping ideas ready-made. The aim is to make good citizens, which is to say, docile and uninquisitive citizens.

—H.L. Mencken

Children who have been diagnosed with a learning disability (delayed reading, dyslexia, dyscalculia, central auditory processing disorder (APD), attention deficit disorder (ADD), or attention deficit hyperactivity disorder (ADHD) often need homeschooling more than others. At home, they can get the time and attention they need, as well as a curriculum that fits their pace and style. Special needs children typically thrive in the homeschooling environment and some learning disabilities have even been shown to diminish and occasionally disappear when learning with a loving parent at home instead of with a teacher in a public school classroom.

Entire books have been dedicated to the topic of homeschooling a learning-disabled child. You should read as many as you can if you are dealing with this situation. Always keep in mind that a diagnosis of any kind of learning disability is not a reason to dismiss the idea of homeschooling—but rather a reason to give it special consideration.

Further Resources on This Topic

Articles, curriculum resources, and tools for help with a variety of learning disabilities
http://www.learningabledkids.com/

Links to multiple special needs homeschooling sites
http://www.homeschoolcentral.com/special.htm

Homeschooling the Child with ADD (or Other Special Needs):
Your Complete Guide to Successfully Homeschooling the
Child with Learning Differences, by Lenore Colacion Hayes

95. How do I start my own homeschooling group if there are none in my region?

Far from failing in its intended task, our educational system is in
fact succeeding magnificently, because its aim is to keep the Ameri-
can people thoughtless enough to go on supporting the system.
　　　　　—Richard Mitchell, *The Underground Grammarian*

As outlined in the book *Asking Questions, Finding Answers* (Home Education Press, 2008), here are the basic steps to starting your own group:

1. Set the Goals of Your Group

Ask yourself what you are looking for in a group. Do you want something that meets often so it doubles as play time for your kids? Do you want it to be parents only? The more you think about before you start, the more you can focus on achieving it. You should ask yourself the following questions:

- Do you want the group to be casual or structured? Are you a group of friends meeting for fun and socializing, or do you have an agenda to meet?
- Will the group be religious or secular? What if someone who is the opposite wants to join your group? Do you want a mix?
- What size should the group be? Both large and small groups have their advantages. If your group ends up being quite big, for example, it may be difficult to find a venue that fits everyone on a regular basis. On the other hand, if it is too small, you may not get the participation and interaction you are looking for.

- How often should the group meet? Weekly? Monthly? What time: in the daytime? evening? weekdays or weekends? For how long each time?
- Where should the group meet? (Keep numbers in mind!)
- Will you charge dues? If so, how much and how will they be used?
- Will you have officers or a structure of leadership?
- Are children allowed at the meetings? You will find that where most homeschoolers go, their children go too, so if you want a support group without kids, you may not get the response you are hoping for.
- What will you call the group? Chances are you are going to do some promoting so it will help to have a clear and memorable name for your group.

2. Market and Promote Your Group

Getting word out about your group is the only way for it to grow and ensure you and your kids are not the only ones in attendance. Some ideas include:

- Write regular newspaper announcements of your meetings and activities.
- Create radio or television community ads (they are often free on local stations).
- List your group on Internet sites (statewide and local).
- Create a website for your group.
- Hold open house at your home or at the chosen venue.
- Offer to speak to churches and other groups.
- Talk to every homeschooler you encounter.
- List your group in magazines such as *Home Education* or *Secular Homeschooling*.
- Initiate and lead local field trips and invite all who show up to join your group.

3. Maintain Your Group

Once you have formed your group and gotten members, you will have to keep up the good work to maintain it. Here are some suggestions:

- Organize a telephone or email tree to remind people about meetings, field trips, and other pertinent information.
- Consistently plan activities to keep people interested.
- Delegate responsibilities to others so that you do not have to shoulder it all and they will feel included.
- Check with other members to make sure their needs are being met. If they are not, find a way to do so.

If you do start your own group, be patient. It takes time, effort, and persistence. Just keep working to create the group you were hoping to find in the first place and it will slowly come together.

Further Resources on This Topic

Submission form for listing your support group online
http://homeschooling.about.com/cs/supportgroups/l/
   blsgprofileform.htm

96. Can my older kids teach my younger ones?

The function of a child is to live his or her own life, not the life that his or her anxious parents think he or she should live, nor a life according to the purpose of the educators who thinks they knows best.
                                        —Alexander Sutherland Neill

Once upon a time, long ago when there were one-room schoolhouses, older children taught younger children every single day. It was considered a normal part of schooling. Today, it is a rather outdated notion—except in homeschooling.

Having your older children work with your younger ones benefits everyone. You, as a parent, benefit because some of your time is freed up to do any of the countless other tasks you had outlined for the day. Your older child benefits because teaching boosts self-esteem and allows for practice of skills already learned. Finally, your younger children benefit because they are being taught by someone who knows and understands them well. The entire family benefits because the bond between members is strengthened. It is a win-win situation for everyone.

Further Resources on This Topic

"Kids Teaching Kids"
http://www.bellaonline.com/articles/art107.asp

"How Children Learn from their Siblings" (not specifically about
     homeschooling, but contains some good advice)
http://www.reallifesolutions.net/family/how-children-learn.html

97. How can I manage all my household duties and homeschool as well?

A family member asked my wife, Aren't you concerned about his (our son's) socialization with other kids? *My wife gave this response:* Go to your local middle school, junior high, or high school, walk down the hallways, and tell me which behavior you see that you think our son should emulate.

—Manfred B. Zysk

When you first consider homeschooling, one item on your list of concerns might be how to do it and still keep up with everything else you are responsible for doing. That is an understandable worry but also one you can easily address. The answer to this is threefold:

1. **It will take less time than you think.** As you already learned earlier in the book, homeschooling takes far less time than you may originally have thought. It rarely takes more than three hours a day, and can often be slipped fairly easily into your schedule, especially since it can be any time of the day.

2. **You will need to learn how to delegate.** If you find yourself running into too much to do and too little time, delegate some of the responsibilities to others: your kids, your partner, your friends and family. Do not try to do everything yourself because chances are you will fall behind, get stressed, and burn out.

3. **You will need to prioritize your responsibilities.** When you begin to homeschool, you will need to make it a priority. That may mean that something else has to be postponed or rescheduled. It may also mean that you need to let things go a little more than you used to—but after all, what is more important than your children's education?

Time management is a skill that takes practice and if you are homeschooling, it may take even more effort. It *is* possible however—so do not give up. There are 24 hours in the day and if you work it right, you might even get to sleep for eight of them!

Further Resources on This Topic

Organization and time management for homeschoolers
http://www.homeschool.com/articles/TimeManagement/default.asp

Advice for the homeschooler on how to manage it all
http://organizedhome.com/time-management-homeschool-families

98. How can I homeschool while traveling?

Public schools are the nurseries of all vice and immorality.
—Henry Fielding

This is far easier than if your children are in public school, because you can take them with you. No more worrying about their missing too many days. No more concern about getting back by a certain date to avoid absenteeism. You can even make traveling a part of your homeschooling curriculum, and unit studies or lessons can almost always be enhanced with road trips.

Wandering around the state or the country can help your kids learn history (museums, monuments, historic homes), science and art (zoos, museums), sports (stadiums, theme parks), and of course a lot of geography. It can also teach lessons about simplicity, teamwork, and family bonds. Since your time is flexible, you can go during the off season and take advantage of discounts on train or plane tickets, hotels, and attraction fees. You can also avoid the crowds!

Traveling is a great way not only to have fun but also to learn. Using travel to enhance your children's education is the perfect combination.

Further Resources on This Topic

Stories and videos about families who homeschool on the road
http://homeschooling.gomilpitas.com/weblinks/traveling.htm

Links to stories and articles about traveling and homeschooling
http://homeschooling.about.com/od/spectraveling/Traveling_
    While_Homeschooling.htm

Videos and stories about families traveling by RV, bicycle,
    and boat
http://www.toadhaven.com/Traveling%20Homeschool%20Families
    .html

Let's Go!

THE END OF this book is only a few pages away. You have learned virtually everything there is to know about homeschooling and soon you will be creating your own stories, tips, suggestions, and anecdotes, and helping others learn about this educational adventure.

Homeschooling Trivia

The Addams Family Homeschool

The first homeschool family on national television was the Addams Family! In the original episode that aired on September 18, 1964, a truant officer arrives at the Addams family house to investigate the fact that Wednesday and Pugsley have never been to school. Gomez is appalled at the idea of regimented schooling, but he gives in, obeying the law. However, Gomez and

Morticia are horrified when Wednesday comes home and they learn that the she is reading Grimm's Fairy Tales and that all of the witches, giants and ogres are killed in the stories. Morticia decides to keep the children home from school because she won't allow the children to learn such things. Gomez demands that Grimm's fairy stories be removed from the curriculum before he'll allow his children to return to school.[1]

------

[1]http://www.knowledgehouse.info/funfacts.html

99. Are all your questions answered?

Educating a child is a natural process. Home schooling is nothing more than an extension of parenting.

—Sue Maakestad

We hope this book and all of its resources helped to answer every question you had. If not, however, do not stop. Keep asking. Keep searching. Read more books. Read homeschooling magazines. Read any of the hundreds of relevant websites. The answers are out there. Some of the most important ones, however, are in your heart and in your children's eyes. Listen to those answers too because sometimes they are the best ones of all.

100. Are you able to do it?

Home schooling is a very old way of doing things. If you look at any of the bills in your wallet or the coins in your pocket, they all have a picture of a homeschooler on them.

—William Lloyd

Of course you are.

Pat yourself on the back. You have been studying, thinking, talking, exploring, and opening your mind to a possible type of education for your family. Whether you do it for a week, a month, a year, or the next ten years, you have succeeded and have made your children's education a priority.

Good for you.

Go to it!

101. Are you ready?

Home is the focus of the work of homeschooling parents. Perhaps like no other challenge in life, homeschooling forces us to consider our identity and our roles as mothers and fathers, and it allows us to shape every aspect of our home—its tone, the way it's decorated, the media we allow to enter it, what we eat and how we eat, how we celebrate, how we laugh, how we rest, and how we prepare for the unexpected.

—Rene Ellison

Of course you are!

You are completely ready.

You have done your homework.

You have talked to your partner.

You have talked to your children.

You know where to start.

You are good to go.

Welcome to the adventure that is homeschooling. Enjoy the journey!

The Ten Top Tens

Books to Read

1. *After Homeschool: Fifteen Teenagers Out in the Real World*, by Tamra Orr
2. *Teenage Liberation Handbook*, by Grace Llewellyn
3. *The Unschooling Handbook*, by Mary Griffith
4. *Teach Your Own*, by John Holt and Patrick Farenga
5. *The Ultimate Book of Homeschooling Ideas*, by Linda Dobson
6. *Home Learning Year by Year*, by Rebecca Rupp
7. *Homeschooling for the Teen Years*, by Cafi Cohen
8. *Homeschooling Our Children, Unschooling Ourselves*, by Alison McKee
9. *Dumbing Us Down: The Hidden Curriculum of Compulsory Schooling*, by John Taylor Gatto
10. *College without High School: A Teenager's Guide to Skipping High School and Going to College*, by Blake Boles

Movies to Watch

1. *Matilda*
2. *Napoleon Dynamite*
3. *Ferris Bueller's Day Off*
4. *The Breakfast Club*
5. *Happy Feet*

6. *The School of Rock*
7. *Charlie Bartlett*
8. *Where the Wild Things Are*
9. *Nim's Island*
10. *Finding Nemo*

People to Know

1. John Holt
2. Charlotte Mason
3. Pat Farenga
4. Raymond and Dorothy Moore
5. Mark and Helen Hegener
6. Linda Dobson
7. Larry and Susan Kaseman
8. Michael Farris
9. Dr. Brian Ray
10. John Taylor Gatto

Websites to Surf

1. A to Z Home's Cool
   http://homeschooling.gomilpitas.com/
2. About Homeschooling
   http://www.homeschooling.about.com
3. Homeschool World
   http://www.home-school.com/
4. Home Education Magazine
   http://www.homeedmag.com/
5. Secular Homeschool
   http://www.secularhomeschool.com/
6. Homeschoolers Connecting
   http://www.homeschoolersconnecting.com/
7. Radical Unschoolers Network
   http://familyrun.ning.com/

8. Growing without Schooling
   http://www.holtgws.com/
9. Family Unschoolers Network
   http://www.unschooling.org/
10. Christian Homeschooling
    http://www.homeschoolchristian.com/

Quotes to Recite

1. *Education is what remains after one has forgotten everything he learned in school.*

   —Albert Einstein

2. *I have never let my schooling interfere with my education.*

   —Mark Twain

3. *An educational system isn't worth a great deal if it teaches young people how to make a living but doesn't teach them how to make a life.*

   —Unknown

4. *Education would be so much more effective if its purpose were to ensure that by the time they leave school every boy and girl should know how much they don't know, and be imbued with a lifelong desire to know it.*

   —Sir William Haley

5. *I am beginning to suspect all elaborate and special systems of education. They seem to me to be built up on the supposition that every child is a kind of idiot who must be taught to think.*

   —Anne Sullivan

6. *Education is an admirable thing, but it is well to remember from time to time that nothing that is worth knowing can be taught.*

   —Oscar Wilde

7. *Much education today is monumentally ineffective. All too often we are giving young people cut flowers when we should be teaching them to grow their own plants.*

   —John W. Gardner

8. *What I hear, I forget. What I see, I remember. What I do, I understand.*

—Confucius

9. *Teaching means different things in different places, but seven lessons are universally taught from Harlem to Hollywood Hills. They constitute a national curriculum you pay for in more ways than you can imagine, so you might as well know what it is. . . . 1. Confusion. 2. Class Position. 3. Indifference. 4. Emotional Dependency. 5. Intellectual Dependency. 6. Provisional Self-Esteem. 7. One Can't Hide. . . . It is the great triumph of compulsory government monopoly mass-schooling that among even the best of my fellow teachers, and among even the best of my students' parents, only a small number can imagine a different way to do things.*

—John Taylor Gatto

10. *I never teach my pupils; I only attempt to provide the conditions in which they can learn.*

—Albert Einstein

Numbers to Know

1. Number of homeschoolers reported in 2008: 1.3 million
2. Percentage of families who state their primary reason for homeschooling is to provide a better education: 48.9
3. Percentage of students enrolled in one or more grade levels above their age-level peers in public school: 25
4. Number of states where it is legal to homeschool: 50
5. Percentage of homeschooled students surveyed who replied they would do it all over again if given the chance: 96
6. Scores on national achievement tests of homeschoolers: 75th–80th percentile
7. Scores on national achievement tests of public schoolers: 50th percentile
8. Increase in the number of homeschoolers receiving National Merit Scholarships over the last decade: 500
9. Percentage of homeschoolers who plan to homeschool their own children: 82

10. Percentage of homeschooled adults who participate in at least one ongoing community service: 71 (percentage of the general population is 37)

States with the Most Homeschoolers
1. California
2. Texas
3. New York
4. North Carolina
5. Florida
6. Illinois
7. Ohio
8. Michigan
9. Georgia
10. New Jersey

Gifts to Request
1. magazine subscriptions
2. museum memberships
3. zoo memberships
4. gift certificates to teacher's supply stores
5. mass transit passes and tickets
6. season tickets to the theater, the symphony, and so forth
7. bookstore gift certificates
8. gasoline gift card
9. computer software
10. board games

Reasons to Homeschool
1. Your child wants to be homeschooled.
2. Your child is struggling in school academically.
3. You believe you can give your child a better education.

4. You are unhappy with the public school system.
5. You want to raise your child with your personal values and morals.
6. You are concerned about incidents of school violence or bullying.
7. You want more time spent together as a family.
8. You want the education to fit your child instead of the reverse.
9. You want to better control and understand what your child is learning.
10. You know that no one will care more about your child and his or her education than you.

Things to Remember

1. Homeschooling is legal in every part of the United States.
2. If you homeschool and change your mind, you can always send your child back to school.
3. If you burn out, you are probably asking too much of someone.
4. Your child has an innate desire to learn; you just need to access it.
5. Homeschooling takes less time than you think.
6. Make the most of your child's learning style.
7. All children are smart—help them realize that.
8. Homeschooling does not have to look anything like public schooling.
9. Learning disabilities improve and even disappear when homeschooling.
10. Homeschooling is growing in every part of the country.

State and National Homeschooling Organizations

National

The Adventist Home Education
PO Box 836
Camino, CA 95709
530-647-2110
http://www.adventisthomeducator.org/

Home School Foundation
PO Box 1152
Purcellville, VA 20134
540-338-8688
www.homeschoolfoundation.org/

Home School Legal Defense Association (HSLDA)
PO Box 3000
Purcellville, VA 20134
540-338-5600
www.hslda.org

National Challenged Homeschoolers Associated Network (NATHHAN)
PO Box 310
Moyie Springs, ID 83845
208-267-6246
http://www.nathhan.com/

National Home Education Research Institute (NHERI)
PO Box 13939
Salem, OR 97309
503-364-1490
www.nheri.org

National Black Home Educators Resource Association
13434 Plank Rd. PMB 110
Baker, LA 70714
225-778-0169
www.nbhe.net/

Support Groups by State

ALABAMA
Christian Home Education Fellowship of Alabama
PO Box 20208
Montgomery, AL 36120
334-288-7229
www.chefofalabama.org

ALASKA
Alaska Private and Home Educators Association (APHEA)
PO Box 141764
Anchorage, AK 99514
907-376-9382
www.aphea.org

ARIZONA
Arizona Families for Home Education (AFHE)
PO Box 2035
Chandler, AZ 85244
602-235-2673
www.afhe.org

ARKANSAS
Believers Homeschool Association
PO Box 11876
Fort Smith, AR 72917
www.homeschoolbelievers.org

CALIFORNIA
California Homeschool Network
PO Box 1061
Mira Loma, CA 91752
800-327-5339
http://californiahomeschool.net/default.htm

Council for Higher Education Accreditation (CHEA®) of California
PO Box 2009
Norwalk, CA 90651
562-864-2432
www.cheaofca.org/

COLORADO
Christian Home Educators of Colorado
10431 South Parker Rd.
Parker, CO 80134
720-842-4852
www.chec.org/

CONNECTICUT

The Education Association of Christian Homeschoolers (TEACH)
10 Moosehorn Rd.
West Granby, CT 06090
860-435-2890
http://www.teachct.org/

DELAWARE

Delaware Home Education Association
PO Box 268
Hartly, DE 19953
http://www.dheaonline.org/

FLORIDA

Florida Parent-Educators Association
255 East Dr., Ste. H
Melbourne, FL 32904
877-275-3732
http://www.fpea.com/

GEORGIA

Georgia Home Education Association (GHEA)
258 Sandy Lake Cir.
Fayetteville, GA 30214
770-461-3657
http://www.ghea.org/

HAWAII

Christian Homeschoolers of Hawaii
c/o 921739 Makakilo Dr., #18
Kapolei, HI 96707
808-689-6398
http://www.christianhomeschoolersof
  hawaii.org

IDAHO

North Idaho Home Educators Association
PO Box 2885
Hayden, IA 83815
http://www.nihea.org/contact.html

ILLINOIS

Illinois Christian Home Educators (ICHE)
PO Box 307
Russell, IL 60075
847-603-1259
http://www.iche.org/

INDIANA

Indiana Association of Home Educators
320 East Main St.
Greenfield, IN 46140
317-467-6244
http://www.inhomeeducators.org/

IOWA

Network of Iowa Christian Home Educators

Box 158

Dexter, IA 50070

800-723-0438 (in Iowa); 515-830-1614 (outside Iowa)

http://www.the-niche.org/

KANSAS

Christian Home Educators Confederation of Kansas

PO Box 1332

Topeka, KS 66601

913-599-0311

http://www.kansashomeschool.org/

KENTUCKY

Christian Home Educators of Kentucky

PO Box 1288

Bardstown, KY 40004

270-358-9270

http://www.chek.org/

LOUISIANA

Christian Home Educators Fellowship of Louisiana Inc.

PO Box 226

Maurice, LA 70555

888-876-2433

http://www.chefofla.org/

MAINE

Association of Homeschoolers of Maine

PO Box 159

Camden, ME 04843

207-763-2880

http://www.homeschoolersofmaine.org/index.htm

MARYLAND

Maryland Association of Christian Home Educators (MACHE)

PO Box 417

Clarksburg, MD 20871

301-607-4284

http://www.machemd.org/

Maryland Home Education Association

9085 Flamepool Way

Columbia, MD 21045

410-730-0073

MASSACHUSETTS

Massachusetts Homeschool Organization of Parent Educators (MASSHOPE)

46 South Rd.

Holden, MA 01520

508-829-0973

http://www.masshope.org/

MICHIGAN

Multiple groups available throughout the
state but best guide is found at:
http://homeschooling.gomilpitas.com/
regional/MichiganSupport.htm

MINNESOTA

**Minnesota Association of Christian
Home Educators (MACHE)**
PO Box 32308
Fridley, MN 55432
763-717-9070 (Metro Area);
866-717-9070 (Greater Metro Area)
http://www.mache.org/

**Minnesota Association of Christian
Home Educators (MHA)**
PO Box 40486
St. Paul, MN 55104
612-288-9662 (Twin City Metro Area);
888-346-7622 (outside Metro Area)
http://www.homeschoolers.org/

MISSISSIPPI

**Mississippi Home Educators
Association (MHEA)**
14290 North Swan Rd.
Gulfport, MS 39503
662-494-1999
http://www.mhea.net/

MISSOURI

Families for Home Education
PO Box 742
Grandview, MO 64030
877-696-6343
http://www.fhe-mo.org/

MONTANA

**Montana Coalition of Home
Educators (MCHE)**
Box 43
Gallatin Gateway, MT 59730
http://www.mtche.org/

NEBRASKA

**Nebraska Christian Home Educators
Association**
PO Box 57041
Lincoln, NE 68505
402-423-4297
http://www.nchea.org/

NEVADA

Nevada Homeschool Network (NHN)
PO Box 1212
Carson City, NV 89702
http://www.nevadahomeschoolnetwork
.com/

NEW HAMPSHIRE

**New Hampshire Homeschooling
Coalition (NHHC)**
PO Box 2224
Concord, NH 03302
603-437-3547
http://www.nhhomeschooling.org/

NEW JERSEY

Education Network of Christian Homeschoolers of New Jersey (ENOCH)
Box 308
Atlantic Highlands, NJ 07716
732-291-7800
http://www.enochnj.org/

New Jersey Homeschool Association
PO Box 1386
Medford, NJ 08055
609-346-2060
http://jerseyhomeschool.net/

NEW MEXICO

Christian Association of Parent Educators-NM
PO Box 3203
Moriarty, NM 87035
505-989-8548
http://www.cape-nm.org/

NEW YORK

Actively and Positively Parenting and Lovingly Educating (APPLE Family and Homeschool Group)
PO Box 2036
N. Babylon, NY 11703
http://www.applenetwork.us/ny/index.html

NORTH CAROLINA

North Carolinians for Home Education
4336-A Bland Rd.
Raleigh, NC 27609
919-790-1100
http://nche.com/

NORTH DAKOTA

North Dakota Home School Association (NDHSA)
1854 107 St. N.E.
Bottineau, ND 58318
701-263-3727
http://ndhsa.org/

OHIO

Christian Home Educators of Ohio
616 Hebron Rd. Ste. E
Heath, OH, 43056
740-522-2460
http://www.cheohome.org/

OKLAHOMA

Home Educators Resource Organization of Oklahoma
12725 Breckenridge Rd.
Enid, OK 73701
http://oklahomahomeschooling.org/

Oklahoma Homeschool Resources (OCHEC)
3801 N.W. 63 St., Bldg 3, Ste. 236
Oklahoma City, OK 73116
405-810-0386
http://www.ochec.com/Categories.aspx?
  Id=HOME

OREGON
Oregon Christian Home Education Association Network
17985 Falls City Rd.
Dallas, OR 97338
503-288-1285
http://www.oceanetwork.org/

Oregon Home Education Network (OHEN)
PO Box 82715
Portland, OR 97282
503-321-5166
http://www.ohen.org/

PENNSYLVANIA
Christian Homeschool Association of Pennsylvanias (CHAP)
231 N. Chestnut St.
Palmyra, PA 17078
717-838-0980
http://www.chaponline.com/

Pennsylvania Home Educators Association
401 Lincoln Ave.
Pittsburgh, PA 15202
http://www.phea.net/

RHODE ISLAND
Rhode Island Guild of Home Teachers
PO Box 432
Coventry, RI 02816
401-996-5991
http://www.rihomeschool.com/

SOUTH CAROLINA
Carolina Homeschooler
PO Box 1421
Lancaster, SC 29721
http://www.carolinahomeschooler.com/

SOUTH DAKOTA
South Dakota Home School Association (SDHSA)
PO Box 882
Sioux Falls, SD 57101
http://www.sdhsa.org

TENNESSEE
Network of Home Education
PO Box 11404
Jackson, TN 38308
http://www.jacksontnhomeschoolers.org/

Tennessee Home Education Association (THEA)
PO Box 681652
Franklin, TN 37068
615-834-3529
http://www.tnhea.org/

TEXAS
Texas Home School Coalition (THSC)
PO Box 6747
Lubbock, TX 79493
806-744-4441
http://www.thsc.org/defaultpage.asp

UTAH
Homeschool Association
PO Box 3942
Salt Lake City, UT 84110
801-296-7198
http://www.utch.org/

VERMONT
Local Homeschool
Vermont Association of Home Educators
1646 E. Albany Rd.
Barton, VT 05822
802-525-4758
www.vermonthoemeschool.org

VIRGINIA
The Organization of Virginia Homeschoolers
PO Box 5131
Charlottesville, VA 22905
866-513-6173
http://www.vahomeschoolers.org/

WASHINGTON
Washington Homeschool Organization
6627 S. 191 Pl., Ste. F-109
Kent, WA 98032
425-251-0439
http://www.washhomeschool.org/

WEST VIRGINIA
Christian Home Educators of West Virginia
PO Box 8770
S. Charleston, WV 25303
877-802-1773
http://www.chewv.org/

WISCONSIN
Christian Home Educators Association (Wisconsin CHEA)
PO Box 320458
Franklin, WI 53132
414-425-6324
http://www.wisconsinchea.com/

Wisconsin Parents Association
PO Box 2502
Madison, WI 53701
608-283-3131
http://homeschooling-wpa.org/

WYOMING
Homeschoolers of Wyoming (HOW)
4859 Palmer Canyon Rd.
Wheatland, WY 82201
307-322-3539
http://www.homeschoolersofwy.org/

Index